RECIPES
FROM
THE RUSSIANS
OF
SAN FRANCISCO

RECIPES FROM THE RUSSIANS OF SAN FRANCISCO

by MARGARET H. KOEHLER

Illustrated by Rudolf Czufin

THE CHATHAM PRESS, INC.

RIVERSIDE, CONNECTICUT

Library of Congress Catalog Card Number: 73-89766
SBN 85699-092-2 (cloth)
SBN 85699-093-0 (paper)

Printed in the United States of America

Also by Margaret H. Koehler:
Recipes from the Portuguese of Provincetown

CONTENTS

ACKNOWLEDGEMENTS

I wish to express very special thanks to my stepmother-in-law, Aline Koehler, who introduced me to the Russians of San Francisco in the first place, and to my brother-in-law, Ronald Koehler, who has shown my husband and me parts of San Francisco and the California coast that I had never before seen, even when living in this section of the country. I also want to thank Mila Dulska, whose way with Russian cooking is pure art; Mrs. Maria Richards, also a "Russian of San Francisco," to whom I am indebted for many of the "facts" about the town's Russian population; and the many other helpful friends I have come to know in the course of discovering and enjoying some of the world's best food.

Христос Воскрес!
(Christ is Risen!)

Воистину Воскрес!
(Verily, He is Risen!)

PREFACE

Although Russian cuisine is not nearly as well known in America as that of many other countries, it deserves stellar rank in the world of cooking. This is true not only of the festive, gourmet dishes but of the everyday ones as well. There is nothing more delicious than serving *bilishi* (Russian hamburgers) for lunch or charcoal broiled *shashlik* for dinner, and most Russian recipes are as simple to prepare as an average American meal would be.

The recipes included in this book were brought to America by Russian immigrants, many of whom arrived here as refugees, carrying with them little but their memories and their traditions. These included recipes of their homeland which, when recreated in their adopted country, evoked nostalgia and helped retain a sense of national identity. The recipes have been passed on from generation to generation, and still are being used today. They have been "Americanized" to the extent that they begin with ingredients which can be found in most grocery stores and supermarkets, but the result loses little or nothing of the flavor of Russia.

Don't let the names dissuade you! As I have collected these recipes over a period of years, some have come my way with the names already translated into English, while others have been in the original Russian — and herein lies a problem. Russia uses the Cyrillic alphabet; English uses the Roman one. Thus in translating back and forth there are bound to be differences in spelling and interpretation.

Piroshki, which are small meat- or fish-filled rolls, for example, can be spelled several different ways. So can *Maslenitza* — the Russian Mardi Gras week — or, for that matter, the famous Russian soup, *borstch*. In accepting a spelling I have gone along either with the experts or with the majority and have tried to be consistent.

But when it comes down to it, the spelling of Russian food names isn't all that important. What *is* important is cooking and eating it. And that adds up to pure pleasure in any language.

I realize, too, that I have given only a sample of Russian cooking, even though there are well over a hundred recipes in this book. Russia is vast and each area has its own cuisine. So I have limited myself to the dishes that the Russians who settled in and around San Francisco brought here with them, from whichever section of the mother country they originally hailed.

MARGARET H. KOEHLER
San Francisco
September, 1973

THE RUSSIANS
OF SAN FRANCISCO

San Francisco is an enchanting city, so naturally dramatic that you have the feeling of living in the middle of a stage set. Nature at its most spectacular provides the scenery, and the cast is made up of a varied and infinitely cosmopolitan population.

San Francisco is, in many ways, an international city, housing colonies of people from all over the world who give it an added dimension, making it seem like many different places at once.

To me, for instance, the Golden Gate City is a combination of the pale amber lights on the Oakland Bay Bridge at night and the gold "onion" domes of a Russian Orthodox Cathedral glistening in the sun; clanging cable cars and a small corner shop which features "take-out piroshki;" sipping cocktails in a lounge hundreds of feet in the sky while staring out at a view that is purely incredible, and responding to vodka toasts at a party where appetizers are called *zakuski* and "Here's to you!" becomes "*Na zdorovie!*" For it is Russian San Francisco that I know best.

Today there are more than 35,000 persons of Russian birth living in the San Francisco Bay area. When you add to this number their children, plus the children of mixed marriages who are at least partly Russian, the figure sharply increases. According to presently available statistics, San Francisco is the most "Russian" city in the United States.

Many of San Francisco's Russians have lived in the area since coming to this country in the early 1920's, in the wake of the Russian Revolution. Still more came after World War II, many of them having been born in cities at the Oriental edge of far-flung Russia like the Pacific port of Vladivostok, or in Manchuria where Harbin, for example, was for years a completely "Russian" city.

Their ultimate arrival in San Francisco was more fitting from an historical viewpoint than most of them realized. For Russia has an historical link with California that goes back for the better part of two centuries. In 1809 the Russians established a settlement at Bodega Bay and by 1812 were erecting a stronghold at Fort Ross, a few miles north of San Francisco, with the intention of building a chain of settlements along the coast to serve as sources of supply for their Alaskan fur trading posts.

In fact, had history gone just a little differently, the Spanish influence so evident in California today might instead have been a Russian one.

Russia's attention originally turned to California before the American Revolution when her Alaskan outposts were faced with a critical shortage of food and a growing scarcity of the fur animals, particularly otter and seal, which were vital to their economy and which were still to be found in large quantities along the California coast.

These operations in the area just north of San Francisco continued until 1841, when the Fort Ross property was sold to Johann August Sutter of Sacramento, who made it the center of a large ranch. The original fort, incidentally, was destroyed in the famous 1906 earthquake and the land was later purchased by the state to be set aside as an historic site. The fort is yet in the process of being restored, an earlier restoration having been severely damaged by fire a few years ago.

So, by the mid-nineteenth century, Russia's "colonial" phase on the West Coast came to an end. But for this, as Louis Adamic pointed out in his book, *A Nation of Nations,* "San Francisco might now be called St. Petersburg or Petrograd; and Los Angeles might be New Moscow or New Vladivostok. The missions now strung the length of California might be bulbous-spired Russian Orthodox Churches."

San Francisco is a city of hills. Approximately fifty-two of them, some small, some large, sprawl from horizon to horizon. Of these, Russian Hill is one of the most famous, and its name derives from the fact that, many years ago, a group of Russian sailors exploring the coast perished and were buried on this hilltop.

San Francisco's Russians, however, have never lived on Russian Hill. Instead, for many years "Little Russia" was the Richmond District in the western part of the city, a wide belt between Golden Gate Park and the Golden Gate itself.

More recently, many Russians have moved "across the park" to the Sunset District, as well as to suburbs throughout the Bay area and to nearby small towns. But Richmond is still heavily Russian in population and remains San Francisco's Russian shopping center.

Geary Boulevard and Clemente Street cut through this district, and the vicinity offers many Russian restaurants, groceries, bakeries, gift shops, delicatessens, book and record stores, and even take-out places which feature such specialties as *borstch* and *piroshki.* They are not always easily recognizable as being "Russian," for many of them have adopted English names. But it is commonplace to hear people chatting in Russian in shops and on street corners here.

The imposing "Holy Virgin Cathedral of the Church in Exile," the largest Russian Orthodox Cathedral in the New World, stands at the corner of 26th Avenue and Geary Boulevard. It was constructed just a few years ago at a cost of several million dollars; money which had been raised entirely by the Russian community.

San Francisco has a daily Russian-language newspaper, *Russian Life,* with a world-wide circulation, as well as many Russian clubs and a Russian Cultural Center which features Russian-language programs.

Like Russians everywhere, the Russians of San Francisco are extremely hospitable people. When they open their doors to a guest it is with a warmth and lavishness that would be hard to surpass.

The dining table is literally the center of the home; the core of family life. Even at a relatively simple dinner it is apt to seem unusually bountiful by American standards. But Russian and American eating habits are quite different. Although the Russians who live in this country have become Americanized in many ways, the majority still prefer their own dining customs. They are not much for quick lunches or TV dinners, although they have learned to resort to these at times for the sake of expediency. Whenever the occasion permits, they would much prefer to linger around the table, sipping coffee and perhaps a glass of sweet wine or a liqueur and enjoying conversation with one another. For Russians are talkative — very vocal, very expressive: there are no sudden moments of silence around a Russian dinner table!

As they did in Old Russia, festivities today still center around church holidays, culminating in the Russian Easter celebration, which is an occasion not only for great joy but for feasting on a scale that staggers the imagination.

Before Easter, however, comes Lent, as solemn a time as Easter is joyous. So to prepare for it, Russians first celebrate a week called *Maslenitza,* which is akin to the French Mardi Gras and means "butter week."

During this whole week "bliny parties" are held in Russian homes. *Bliny* are pancakes which should be made with yeast but no longer always are. Today's Americanized Russians often use mixes, especially the buckwheat varieties.

Toward the end of *Maslenitza,* fancy costume balls are held. This is one of the few times when Russians are apt to wear the beautiful, colorful costumes for which they are famous — swirling skirts for the women, dashing satin blouses for the men. It has been many years, even in Russia itself, since this sort of dress has been worn for anything other than "masquerades."

Maslenitza comes to an end on a Sunday and Lent begins the following day. There is no Ash Wednesday in the Russian Orthodox Church. Lent, especially among the older people, is very strict, with quite a bit of fasting. It is an especially tantalizing period for those who like to eat — and most Russians do — because, especially during the latter part of it, special foods are constantly being prepared for Easter.

As Easter approaches, the Russian stores in San Francisco outdo themselves in the splendor of their window decorations. They feature the huge *kulich*, the traditional Russian Easter cake, which is festooned with candy roses, chickens and bunnies; armies of chocolate animals wrapped in rainbow-hued foil; and all sorts of fancy cookies and small cakes.

Russian Easter eggs, decorated in many styles and colors, are so tempting that it becomes almost impossible to choose among them. The style of decoration usually depends upon the section of Russia from which the decorator came. Some are wooden eggs enameled in intricate geometric patterns, with red, black and yellow as the predominant colors, or painted with pastels and decorated with flowers. Some are beautifully fragile real eggs, the contents having been blown out of the shells through pinholes, the shells then lavishly painted, sequined or jeweled. Decorated Easter eggs are a true Russian art form and have been since masters of the craft long ago fashioned them for the tsars, using magnificent precious jewels as adornments.

Inside the bakeries and delicatessens there are huge *pirogs* for sale, whole or by the piece. These are large pies with yeast-dough crusts and fillings of chopped eggs, meat, cabbage, mushrooms or fish. There are also many varieties of *piroshki*, the "little brother" of the *pirog*. *Piroshki* are as basically Russian as *borstch* and look somewhat like oval dinner rolls, with the surprise in the meat, fish and other fillings. And there are pastries of all kinds.

There are rows and rows of sugar roses in various sizes and colors to be purchased and used as decoration on a homemade *kulich*. There are stacks of huge meringues, especially plentiful now because it is a good way to use up the astronomical number of egg whites left over from making a *kulich,* in which are used only the yolks. All the makings for an infinite variety of *zakuski* are at hand, plus special chocolates, wines and liqueurs.

Easter is the culmination when, once the final Mass has been said, the feasting and visiting begins. There is warmth, love and a beautiful feeling of brotherhood to a Russian Easter. Open house is the order of the day, and people visit from one home to another, touched with a special kind of elation. It is customary to embrace friends and strangers alike, kissing them first on each cheek and then on the mouth.

Easter feasting goes on from house to house; there seems to be no end to it, nor to the Russians' capacity to enjoy it. The traditional Easter greeting is repeated again and again — *Christos Voskres!,* which means "Christ Is Risen!" Then the response is given: *Voistinu Voskres!,* which means "Truly He Is Risen!"

The center of the festivity is the elaborate buffet on the dining room table. There are all sorts of *zakuski* — eggplant caviar, red caviar, black caviar, herring, creamed mushrooms, thinly sliced radishes in sour cream, probably a liver *pashtet,* which is a kind of pâté, and on and on and on. Then there are usually plates of cold sliced turkey and ham, an assortment of breads, colored hard boiled eggs, fancy cookies of many kinds and, of course, well chilled vodka — though many of the Russians today have switched their preference to American-style highballs or wine.

Dominating the table are the two symbols of Russian Easter; the *kulich* and the *paskha.* To a Russian it just wouldn't be Easter without a slice of *kulich,* which has a rich, buttery, coffee-cake-like texture and is studded with glazed fruit, and without a mound of *paskha,* a creamy cottage-cheese concoction which is made and decorated in a variety of ways.

In shape, both the *kulich* and the *paskha* follow tradition. The *kulich* is tall and rounded at the top to symbolize the onion-shaped dome of a Russian church. Sometimes it is lavishly decorated; sometimes it is quite simple. But usually written in icing on the top or on one side are the initials X B. X is the equivalent in the Cyrillic alphabet of the Roman Ch. B is the Cyrillic equivalent of V. Thus, these two initials stand for *Christos Voskres.*

The traditional *paskha* is shaped like a pyramid, and there is a special mold in which to make it. The older molds are wooden, sometimes having been passed down within families, and may be well over a hundred years old. Today there are plastic versions available, which are made locally and sell for a few dollars.

Certainly no people in the world love holidays *more* than the Russians do, and probably few love them quite as much. Russians celebrate the American Thanksgiving, for instance, from their first year in this country. As might be expected, they tend to do it with a Russian accent. They start out with a few *zakuski* and then indulge in conventional turkey-with-all-the-trimmings; but they stop when it comes to pumpkin pie. It is dangerous to generalize about Russia because it is such a huge country, encompassing so many cultures, but for the most part, Russians simply do not like pumpkin. At least, the Russians of San Francisco don't; this is one of the few American foods which they have not adopted.

Christmas is also a time of feasting, with cakes and cookies in abundance and lots of nuts, raisins, grapes, apples and oranges on hand. Goose is a favorite for Christmas dinner.

In addition to holidays, tradition is still staunchly upheld in the major events of family life. Russian weddings, for instance, are very traditional, beginning with a lengthy Orthodox church ceremony.

A bride's family does not necessarily pay for the wedding. In fact, if the groom's family is well off, it is more likely that they will pay, while sometimes both families share the expenses. The principal consideration is the wedding itself rather than the cost of it or who defrays the cost.

If the reception is held in a public place, it is apt to be "Americanized," perhaps with a full-course, sit-down dinner served. But if it is held in the home, it will almost certainly be Russian, consisting of a lavishly decorated buffet with many kinds of *zakuski,* sliced lamb, turkey and ham with champagne first and later vodka.

Here again, it is risky to generalize about Russians, but "wedding cakes," at least as we know them, are not Russian. In older times, *plombir,* an elaborate frozen dessert, was traditional at weddings and was served with an assortment of small cakes and cookies. Now, however, the tiered, white-frosted, American-style wedding cake complete with bells or a miniature bride and groom is a part of every Russian wedding reception, simply because this is an American touch the Russians like!

Birthday cakes are not Russian, either. A *pirog* is traditional fare for this celebration. It may be made with any one of a variety of fillings, and is cut in wedge-shaped slices and served with tea or coffee. Cookies and desserts usually follow.

When someone moves into a new house, friends always give him bread and salt, or they may substitute a cake today for the bread. But bread and salt are considered by Russians to be the most necessary, really basic things in life, and the gift is to make sure that the recipient will always have these vital items.

Russians tend to make their home their social focal point; and perhaps this is why there are not more Russian restaurants in the United States. There are a number of good ones in San Francisco and New York and, to a lesser extent, in other American cities, but in comparison to places featuring the cuisine of other nationalities, they are few and far between. For many people, the only way to a good Russian dinner is to make it themselves!

Fortunately, this is entirely possible and not difficult. The ingredients used in Russian cooking are easily obtainable. Even *kasha,* which used to be available only in specialty stores, is now sold in supermarkets everywhere, often under the name "buckwheat groats." And most American kitchens contain all the pots and pans that would be necessary to prepare anything Russian. No special dishes or utensils are needed except, perhaps, a *paskha* mold if you go all out for tradition.

Also, there is a practical side to the Russian nature: Russian-American women take full advantage of convenience foods and use mixes, frozen foods and whatever else is available. In making these adaptations, however, they make sure to retain the original flavor.

Although at first glance it may seem that the Russians do not use herbs and spices extensively, do not be misled into thinking that, because of this, their cooking is bland. Rather, it is unusually flavorful. Spices were first used because they were excellent food preservatives and, even today, they are especially featured in the cuisine of countries with warm climates such as Italy, Spain or Mexico. The Russians particularly favor dill, whether fresh, in dry seed form or in pickles, as well as bay leaves, horseradish, dry mustard, parsley and garlic. They use mushrooms, onions and cabbage plentifully, and when their dishes are blended with sour cream, all of these underlying flavors are enhanced. Soy sauce is also very popular, especially with those Russians who lived in Siberia and China before coming to this country. It goes very well with Russian food, and a dash of it is often added to give zest, for example, to meat loaf or various fillings.

San Francisco's Russian cooking has come to be regarded as some of the finest Russian cooking in the world today, for good reason. It blends the best of the old and the best of the new. There is nothing dull about Russian food!

TO SET THE MOOD
— Zakuski

The only problem with *zakuski*, which is the Russian way of saying hors d'oeuvres, is that they are so good! It is very difficult not to eat too many of them and spoil the appetite for the delicious dinner that is sure to follow.

There is an almost endless number of recipes for Russian *zakuski*. They are, and long have been, the traditional beginning to any Russian meal except, perhaps, afternoon tea. In her book, *Dining and Wining in Old Russia*, (E. P. Dutton: 1933), Nina Nikolaevna Selivanova, a Russian noblewoman who came to this country after the First World War, painted a vivid word picture of the part food, especially *zakuski*, played in the Russian social life of the past. Describing the monthly banquet for the officers and their families at one of the Guards regiments in St. Petersburg, Mme. Selivanova writes:

As soon as dinner was announced everybody proceeded to the library where a long, long table was set, covered with a beautiful white tablecloth, which completely disappeared under the array of dishes, plates, silver, wine bottles, glasses, etc. Flowers occupied the middle of the table, from one end to the other, except for a space in the very center: there stood a barrel of opaque glass at least 20 inches high, filled with fresh caviar — for this long table was the *zakuski* table and there were about a hundred varieties of them dispersed about the table, the cold ones in cut glass dishes of all sizes and shapes; the hot ones in silver or nickel, copper or glass baking dishes, each one covered to preserve both the warmth and the fragrance.

Twenty to thirty varieties of sweetened and bitter vodkas were served with the *zakuski* and sometimes even more. In those days a Russian would easily sample some forty to fifty *zakuski* while sauntering about as he selected his favorite ones and would drink about twenty small vodka glasses of different vodkas. Then, after even the smallest eater had partaken of enough *zakuski* to feed a large family for an entire week, they passed into the dining room to eat a nine course dinner. But in order to revive their appetites, they stopped in an adjoining room and drank a glass of English ale which has — so it is said — the extraordinary capacity of making one hungry after one has just eaten.

Life is simpler today, and it would seem that appetites are smaller, too. *Zakuski* are no longer served on such a large scale, but even so, the assortment of *zakuski* at a Russian party can be dazzling. Sometimes they are served buffet style; other times the guests sit around the dining table, munch *zakuski* for an hour or more and sip vodka. Soup and *piroshki* follow as a next course, and then perhaps a roast and some vegetables, the whole terminating — much later — with dessert, coffee and liqueurs. For most diet-conscious Americans, this is really too much!

I much prefer to serve my *zakuski* buffet style and offer vodka with them. You don't have to drink vodka, but it *is* the perfect accompaniment to *zakuski*. It is usually served in a crystal decanter or similar type of carafe, which is filled with vodka and then refrigerated until serving time. The vodka must be very well chilled — really cold. The individual servings are then offered in small liqueur or other decorative, shot-sized glasses.

Most *zakuski* are quite easy to prepare, and almost all of the varieties may be made in advance and refrigerated. I often make mine the day before I intend to use them and store them in plastic ice cream cartons. Then I mix each one well before turning it out into a cut glass (the Russian way) or other attractive serving dish. I serve them accompanied by rye and pumpernickel breads — the small, "party" sizes do very well, or the regular-sized slices may be used quartered. Melba toast or crackers, especially those with a touch of rye or pumpernickel, also go well. You can dip many of the *zakuski*, or simply spread them on bread and eat them with the fingers. But the Russian way is to furnish small plates and forks and let each person make his own assortment.

Because *zakuski* are so tempting, I have adopted my own rule of thumb when it comes to serving them. I plan one kind of *zakuski* for every two guests and perhaps throw in an extra one for good measure. This means that if you are having eight people for dinner, you can plan on four or five different varieties. The selection is a matter of individual taste. Personally, I prefer to serve cold *zakuski* and reserve the warm ones, such as creamed mushrooms, for luncheon — but again, it is a matter of taste.

EGGPLANT CAVIAR

1 large eggplant

1 medium onion

½ cup olive oil

1 tablespoon lemon juice

Salt and pepper to taste

Bake the eggplant, whole, in a 400°F. oven until it is soft, about 30 to 45 minutes. It will be done when you can easily pierce it with a fork. Let cool. Remove the skin and chop the meat very fine leaving in the seeds. Grate the onion and add it to the meat, along with the olive oil, salt, pepper and lemon juice. Mix together and chill well before serving.

My own touch with eggplant caviar is something that I have found works well with many *zakuski*: use a blender. I cut the baked and peeled eggplant into fairly large pieces, put them in the blender with the other ingredients and let it whirl just until everything is well mixed. For a long time I wondered why the Russians called this "caviar." But the eggplant seeds do look like caviar and give the same kind of texture. For that reason, don't overblend.

RADISHES IN SOUR CREAM

Radishes   **Salt and pepper**

Sour cream

Select large, firm radishes, wash them well and then chill them
thoroughly. Slice them very thin and blend with sour cream, so that
it has the consistency of a thick sauce. Salt and pepper to taste. (One
bunch of radishes goes a long way.) Chill well before serving.

LIVER BUTTER-CHEESE

½ **pound calves' liver or**   **2 tablespoons mild cheddar**

   chicken livers   **cheese, grated**

Butter, approximately 1 cup

Cook the liver, cool it and then put it through a meat grinder.
Measure the meat and add an equal amount of butter — that is to say,
for 1 cup of ground liver, add 1 cup of butter. Add the grated cheese
and work the mixture until it is smooth and even. Chill well before
serving.

LIVER PASHTET

6 to 8 raw chicken livers

½ pound bacon

½ cup hot olive oil

Juice of 1 lemon

1 cup cooked chicken meat

Small slice of smoked ham

3 apples

½ pound mushrooms

¼ pound butter

3 eggs

4 tablespoons chicken bouillon

1 cup flour

1 tablespoon butter

1 cup sour cream

Grated cheese for topping

Salt and pepper to taste

Wash the chicken livers well and put them through a meat grinder with half the bacon. Place this mixture in a bowl and pour the olive oil and lemon juice over it. Set aside.

Chop the chicken, ham, apples and mushrooms. (The all-white-meat chicken sold in cans and jars is perfectly satisfactory for this.) Season to taste. Melt the butter and beat the eggs and chicken bouillon into it. Add the flour and mix the egg-flour mixture with the chicken-ham mixture. This forms a "stuffing."

Butter an 8-inch round or rectangular baking dish. Pour in the sour cream and spread it out evenly. Sprinkle this with grated cheese. Alternate layers of half the stuffing mixture, half the chicken-liver mixture, the remainder of the stuffing, and finish with the remainder of the liver mixture. Put the remainder of the bacon in strips across the top. This may be baked as is or topped with a thin layer of pie crust, if desired. Bake at 375°F for 30 minutes. It may be served hot or cold.

MY OWN "RUSSIAN LIVER PÂTÉ"

1 family-size can liver paste or
   liverwurst spread
½ pint sour cream

1 dill pickle, chopped
Salt and pepper

I had asked some guests over for cocktails and *zakuski* one night and wanted to give them a good assortment since Russian food was new to them. But I realized that I wasn't going to have the time to make an authentic Russian liver paté, so I improvised.

I had on hand a family-size can of liverwurst spread, which I turned out into a bowl and beat thoroughly with a fork. Then I beat sour cream into it until it had a thick, smooth consistency. (You may not wish to use the entire half pint of sour cream; it is a matter of preference.) To this I added about half a large dill pickle, finely chopped, and some salt and pepper. I turned the mixture into a cut glass dish, garnished it with the remainder of the pickle, chopped rather coarsely, and let it chill. The result was not only very good — it was also very Russian! It is now a standard *zakuski* at our house, and is a recipe I've been happy to share with Russian friends in San Francisco.

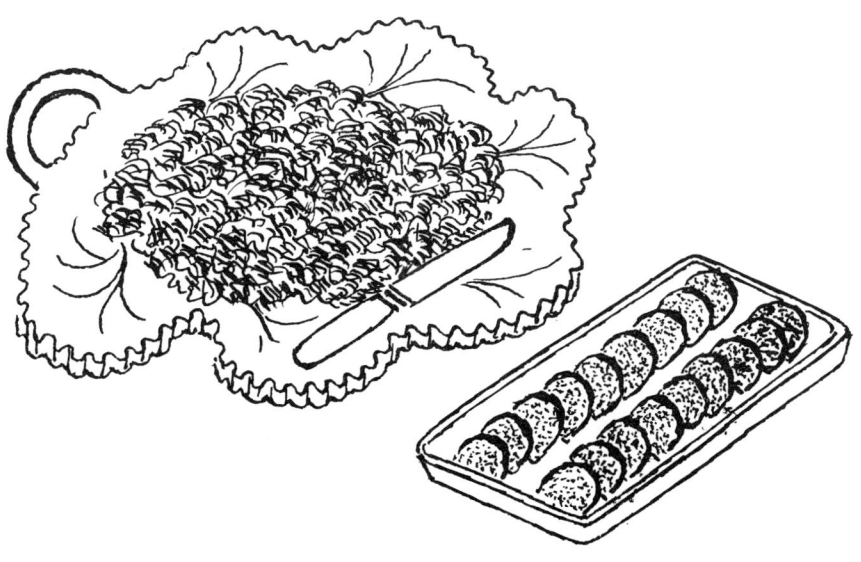

CAVIAR AND SOUR CREAM

1 3-ounce jar black or red (salmon) caviar	3 ounces cream cheese
	½ pint sour cream
1 tablespoon lemon juice	1 tablespoon onion, finely grated

It would be nice if we could all have "fresh Beluga caviar," but for most of us it is beyond reach, both in price and availability. So, long ago, I learned to make do with the caviar available in supermarkets, and whether you select a "lumpfish" or "whitefish" roe, or the eye-pleasing pink salmon roe, a delicious *zakuski* can be produced from it very easily.

First chill the caviar. Turn it out into a dish and thin it with the lemon juice (it can be the bottled variety). This tends to cut the oiliness in the black caviar and adds a zesty flavor to the salmon.

In a separate bowl work the cream cheese, which should be at room temperature, until it is smooth and then gradually add enough sour cream to approximate the consistency of very thick whipped cream. (It probably will not take the entire half pint.) Blend in the onion.

Spread the cream cheese-sour cream mixture evenly into a cut glass or other attractive serving dish. Then top it with the caviar, spooning it in carefully so that there is no blending. Chill. When served, the caviar and cream does get mixed, and it goes particularly well with melba toast rounds.

PICKLED MUSHROOMS

1 pound or 1 large package
  fresh mushrooms
1 tablespoon mixed pickling
  spices

1 pint vinegar
2 onions, chopped
1 teaspoon pepper

Wash the mushrooms. Depending upon their size, they may be used whole or sliced. Boil them in salted water for about 10 minutes, then drain. Boil the vinegar, pickling spices, chopped onions and pepper for 5 minutes. Let the mixture cool. Pack the mushrooms into a quart jar, cover them with the vinegar mixture and let stand at least overnight. Refrigerate for several days before using them, turning the jar upside down occasionally so that the pickling mixture circulates.

Here again I must admit that I have a short cut. I buy canned button mushrooms, the biggest ones I can get, and pack them in a jar. Over this I pour bottled Italian salad dressing. It produces a very Russian-type mushroom! I refrigerate the jar for at least 3 days before using the mushrooms, which improve with age.

CREAMED MUSHROOMS

1 pound fresh mushrooms	Hot water for thinning
2 tablespoons butter	Salt and pepper
1 scant tablespoon flour	½ pint sour cream

Coarsely chop the mushrooms and sauté them in butter until golden brown. Sprinkle the flour over them and then add enough hot water to make a medium-thick sauce. Season with salt and pepper, stir in enough sour cream to reach the desired thickness, and heat thoroughly. These may be served hot as a *zakuski;* or you can make the sauce a little thinner and serve it over a meat loaf, thus giving the meat a decidedly Russian accent. The mushrooms also make an excellent luncheon dish over toast or noodles.

GREEN BEAN SALAD

½ cup sugar

½ cup olive or corn oil

⅓ cup vinegar (approximately)

2 16-ounce cans blunt-cut
    green beans

1 teaspoon paprika

1 purple onion, thinly sliced

4 tablespoons sour cream

Put the sugar and oil in a measuring cup and add enough vinegar to make 1 full cup of liquid. Drain the beans and pour the liquid over them. Sprinkle with paprika. Put the thinly sliced onions on top, cover the bowl with foil or plastic wrap and let it stand in the refrigerator overnight. Before serving, pour off all the juice and remove the onions. Add the sour cream, stir in well and serve. (The Russian way is to remove the onions, but they may be blended in with the other ingredients, if preferred.)

BEET RELISH

1 8-ounce can or jar beets

1 small onion

1 small jar horseradish

1 tablespoon sugar

1 teaspoon salt

Vinegar to taste

Grate the beets coarsely and grate the onion finely. Mix the grated beets and onion with the horseradish, sugar and salt, and add vinegar to taste. Store in the refrigerator in a glass jar until ready to serve. The flavors improve as they blend. A jar of ready-prepared chopped or sliced pickled beets, well chilled, also makes a perfectly acceptable *zakuski*.

SAUERKRAUT, RUSSIAN STYLE

1 pound fresh or canned sauerkraut	1 tablespoon salad oil
	1 tablespoon dry mustard
1½ tablespoons sugar	½ small onion, sliced

Drain the sauerkraut. If canned sauerkraut is used, wash it thoroughly in cold water and drain it again. Mix the sugar, oil, mustard and onion together and blend with the sauerkraut. Chill until served. Sauerkraut is very popular with the Russians, incidentally, and they use it in many ways.

SAUERKRAUT SALAD

1 pound fresh or canned sauerkraut	½ cup vegetable oil
	2 tablespoons vinegar
2 tablespoons dill pickle, chopped	2 teaspoons mustard
	3 to 5 lettuce leaves
¼ cup cucumbers, diced	Salt and pepper to taste
1 cup cooked beets, diced	2 hard boiled eggs, sliced

Soak the sauerkraut in cold water to cover for ½ hour. Drain until all possible water has been removed from it, and chop. Mix with all the other ingredients except the lettuce and hard boiled eggs. Make a bed of the lettuce leaves, spoon the sauerkraut mixture onto it and decorate it with the egg slices. This may be served as a cold vegetable or salad course, as well as a *zakuski*.

MOSCOW SELIANKA

1 pound fresh or canned
  sauerkraut
1 tablespoon sugar
1 onion
¼ pound butter
2 cups cooked veal, ham or
  chicken, sliced

1 dill pickle, sliced
8 to 10 green olives and 8 to 10
  mushrooms, fresh or pickled
Salt and pepper

If canned sauerkraut is used, rinse it first in cold water, then drain. Cover the sauerkraut with water and cook for about 20 minutes, or until tender. Add the sugar and cook for 5 more minutes. Drain. Chop the onion and sauté it in butter until light brown and translucent. Add the sauerkraut and let the mixture simmer for a few minutes. Place half the sauerkraut in a well-greased baking dish and top it first with the slices of meat (this is a good way to use up leftovers), then with half of the pickle slices and a few mushrooms and olives. Add the rest of the sauerkraut, top with the rest of the pickle, more mushrooms and olives. Season to taste. Bake at 400°F for about 30 minutes and serve hot.

FISH SELIANKA

1 pound fresh or canned
   sauerkraut
1 tablespoon sugar
1 pound filet of white fish, any
   kind
1 onion, chopped

¼ pound butter
1 dill pickle, sliced
8 to 10 green olives and 8 to 10
   mushrooms, fresh or pickled
Salt and pepper

If the sauerkraut is canned, wash it thoroughly in cold water, then drain. Cover the sauerkraut with water and cook for about 20 minutes, or until tender. Add the sugar and cook 5 minutes more. Drain. Fry the fish filets and the chopped onion in some of the butter until nicely browned. Put half the sauerkraut in a buttered casserole, top with the fish, sprinkle with the pickle slices, add the remainder of the sauerkraut and top with the mushrooms and olives. Salt and pepper to taste. Bake at 375°F for about 25 minutes. Serve hot.

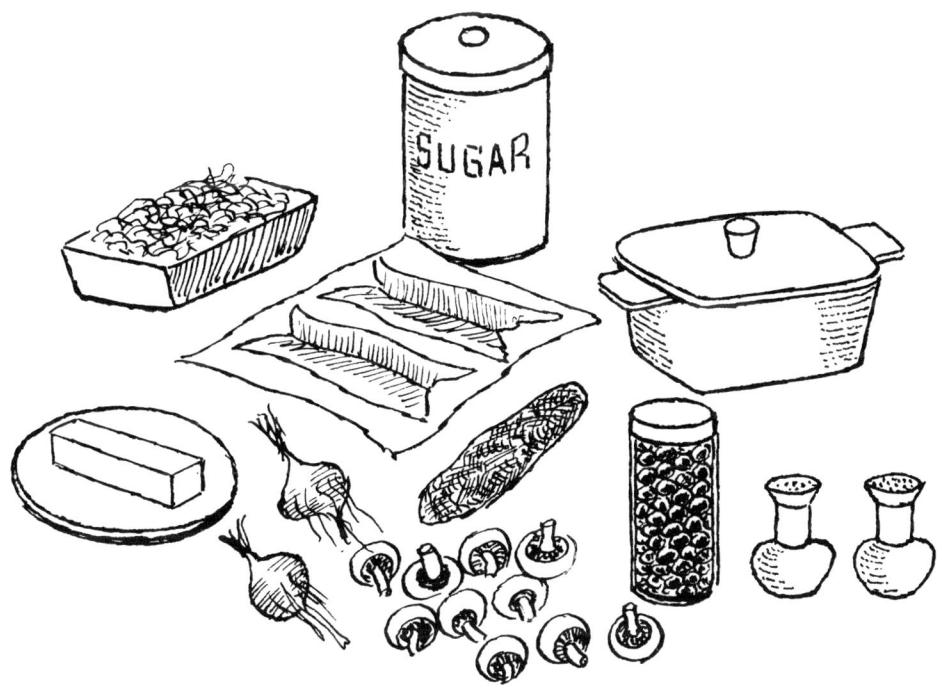

ROQUEFORT BUTTER-CHEESE

¼ pound roquefort cheese
¼ pound butter

¼ cup walnuts or pecans, chopped

Grate the cheese and mix it with the butter until it is smooth and even. Blend in the nuts. Any kinds of cheese and nuts may be used for this kind of *zakuski*.

ANCHOVY BUTTER-CHEESE

10 anchovy filets (canned)
1 onion, chopped

1 apple
½ pound butter

Put the anchovies, onion and apple through a meat grinder together. Blend them with the butter until the mixture is smooth and even. Chill until ready to serve.

CHOPPED HERRING

1 8-ounce jar pickled herring filets
1 small apple, finely chopped

1 tablespoon butter
Parsley or dill for garnish
1 hard boiled egg, sliced

Chop the herring until it is quite fine, or whirl it in the blender. Add the finely chopped (or blended) apple and the butter, mixing together thoroughly. Turn into a dish and garnish with the sliced egg and sprigs of parsley or dill. Chill until ready to serve.

STUFFED EGGS

6 eggs, hard boiled

1 3-ounce jar black caviar

2 teaspoons lemon juice
(or to taste)

Slice the eggs in half lengthwise and remove the yolks. Crumble them with a fork and set aside. Fill the egg white cavities with caviar and then sprinkle lightly with lemon juice. Mound a little of the crumbled yolk in the center of each one and chill until serving time.

EGGS WITH HORSERADISH

6 eggs, hard boiled

½ cup mayonnaise

½ cup sour cream

1 tablespoon horseradish

Salt and pepper to taste

Paprika for garnish

Chop the eggs coarsely, toss lightly with the other ingredients, pour into a cut glass or other attractive serving dish and decorate with a little paprika. Chill until serving time.

CUCUMBERS WITH SOUR CREAM

3 cucumbers

2 hard boiled eggs

¼ cup sour cream

¼ teaspoon vinegar

Dry mustard,

Sugar,

Salt and pepper to taste

Peel the cucumbers and cut them into chunks. Coarsely chop the eggs and then mix with the cucumbers. In a separate bowl, make a dressing of the sour cream, vinegar, mustard, sugar, salt and pepper to taste. Add a little more vinegar and sugar to the dressing if it does not seem thin enough. Toss lightly with the cucumbers and eggs, then chill until serving time.

VINIGRET

1 large beet	3 tablespoons olive oil
3 potatoes	2 tablespoons vinegar
¼ pound string beans	Salt and pepper to taste
2 dill pickles, coarsely chopped	Chopped parsley for garnish
1 stalk celery, chopped	

Boil the whole beet, potatoes and string beans together until the beet is tender when pierced with a fork, about 20 to 30 minutes. Cool, then peel and cut everything into small pieces. Add the pickles and the celery. Mix with the olive oil, vinegar and salt and pepper. Sprinkle with parsley and chill until ready to serve.

SHRIMP VINIGRET

½ pound cooked fresh or frozen shrimp or 1 large can shrimp	2 dill pickles or 1 fresh cucumber
1 large beet	6 green olives, sliced
3 potatoes	Mayonnaise to taste
2 carrots	2 hard boiled eggs

Wash the shrimp in cold water, drain and set aside. Boil the beet, potatoes and carrots, whole, until the beet is fork tender, or about 20 to 30 minutes. Cool, peel the beet and potatoes, and cut everything into small pieces. Add the cucumber or the pickles, the olives and the shrimp. Gently toss with mayonnaise to taste. Chill until ready to serve. Garnish with sliced hard boiled eggs.

TOMATO SALAD

6 large tomatoes	Salt and pepper to taste

Sauce

1 tablespoon dry mustard	1 egg yolk
1 tablespoon sugar	1 tablespoon vinegar
2 tablespoons olive oil	

Slice the tomatoes, or chop them coarsely, and add salt and pepper to taste. Make the sauce by stirring the mustard and sugar into the oil, heating it, then gradually beating in the egg yolk. Mix well, add the vinegar, let simmer for a few minutes and pour over the tomatoes. Chill well before serving.

STUFFED TOMATOES

2 hard boiled eggs, yolks only	1 3-ounce jar black caviar
2 dozen cherry tomatoes	2 dozen toast rounds, buttered

Remove the yolks from the eggs and mash finely with a fork or put them through a sieve. Set aside. Cut a thin slice from the base of each tomato. Carefully scoop out the pulp, then turn the tomato upside down and let it drain. Stuff the tomatoes with caviar and put each, cut side down, on a buttered toast round. Sprinkle the egg yolk around the base of each tomato to form a border.

MILA'S TOMATOES

Several large tomatoes or   1 sprig dill
   1 carton cherry tomatoes   1 cup salt
1 to 2 cloves garlic   1 cup vinegar

This recipe from Mila Dulska may be served either as a *zakuski* or as a main course accompaniment. It is not only delicious but surprisingly refreshing. The cherry tomatoes are particularly nice for *zakuski*, although Mila uses large, whole ones. Whatever size you select, puncture the tomatoes here and there with a fork and pack them into a jar, adding a sprig of dill and a clove or two of peeled garlic to each jar. Cover with a hot mixture made in a proportion of 13 cups of water to 1 cup of salt and 1 cup vinegar which has been brought to a boil and cooled slightly. Store in the refrigerator; they keep indefinitely.

RUSSIAN POTATO SALAD

1 pint potato salad   1 small onion, chopped
1 cup pickled beets, diced   Salt and pepper
1 small dill pickle, finely diced   2 hard boiled eggs

Buy prepared potato salad for this, available in most supermarkets and delicatessens. Mix the potato salad with the beets, pickle, onion and one of the eggs, chopped. Salt and pepper to taste. Turn out into an attractive cut glass serving dish, garnish with the remaining egg, sliced, and chill until ready to serve. This has a very pretty rosy color and a delicious flavor.

RUSSIAN SOUPS
Meals In Themselves

Borstch is, without question, the most famous of the Russian soups, even though it is not a single soup at all. The word means "beet soup," and there are dozens of varieties of it, every section of that vast land that is Russia having its own recipes which vary, to some extent, not only from village to village but from household to household.

Borstch can be a simple beet-based soup suitable for a first course, or it can be a hearty meal in a pot, loaded with meat, potatoes and vegetables. Occasionally, the Russians do serve a cold *borstch*, but more often it is served hot. The cold beet *borstch* available in jars in most delicatessens and supermarkets is really more Jewish in origin than Russian.

I notice that when Russians serve *borstch* as a first course at dinner, they usually choose a simple *borstch* made with meat stock but from which the meat itself has been removed. A small serving of this, delicious though it is, is usually enough when you consider the dishes that will follow, and when you have probably already partaken of several *zakuski!*

I personally feel that a hearty *borstch* is a full meal in itself, and deserves the stellar role at the table. It makes a wonderful Sunday night supper. First, serve a few *zakuski.* Then serve big steaming bowls of *borstch* accompanied by pumpernickel or rye bread and unsalted butter. Top this off with cheese and crackers, fresh fruit and coffee, and even the fussiest gourmet must admit that it was a great repast.

Borstch is by no means the only kind of soup the Russians eat, even though the other varieties are not as well known outside the Russian community. Any of the other soups may also be served as a first course, but keep the portions small: they, too, can be deliciously, but surprisingly, filling.

BORSTCH

2 pounds stew beef and bone
1 stalk celery, sliced
1 onion, sliced
1 bay leaf
3 potatoes, diced coarsely
Salt and pepper to taste
1 green pepper, sliced

4 to 5 beets, washed but not
  peeled
2 carrots, sliced
3 tomatoes or 1 16-ounce can
  tomatoes
1 6-ounce can tomato sauce
2 teaspoons sugar

Put all the ingredients except the tomatoes, tomato sauce and sugar in a deep pot. Cover with water and cook, covered, for 3 hours. Do this the day before you intend to serve the *borstch*.

Store the soup overnight in the refrigerator. When ready to serve, remove the fat from the surface and take out the soup bone, the meat and the beets. Cut the meat into bite-size pieces, peel the beets and cut them into thin strips, and return the meat and beets to the soup mixture. Add the tomatoes, cut into large pieces, and the tomato sauce. Add salt and pepper to taste and the sugar. Bring to a boil and let simmer for about 15 minutes. Pass sour cream in a separate bowl and stir a heaping spoonful into each dish of soup. Also serve fresh dill as a garnish, if available. *Serves 8 to 10*

BORSTCH, ODESSA STYLE

1½ pounds soup meat and a
marrowbone
1 onion, sliced thinly
1 small cabbage, shredded finely
1 cup diced carrots
½ cup celery, finely sliced
1 green pepper, thinly sliced

6 fresh or whole canned
tomatoes, peeled and
quartered
3 beets, cooked, peeled and
sliced
Salt and pepper to taste

Put the soup meat and marrowbone in a large, deep pot. Cover the
meat with cold water and cook, covered, for about 1 hour. Strain the
stock and remove the meat. (Later you can slice the meat and brown
it in butter, add mushrooms and cook until they are nicely browned,
then stir in sour cream, salt and pepper to taste, and you will have a
delicious Russian luncheon dish.)

Add the onion, cabbage, carrots and celery to the meat stock. Simmer, covered, for 30 minutes, then add the green pepper, tomatoes,
beets and the water in which the beets were cooked. Cook for another
30 minutes. Serve with a spoonful of sour cream stirred into each bowl
of soup. *Serves 6*

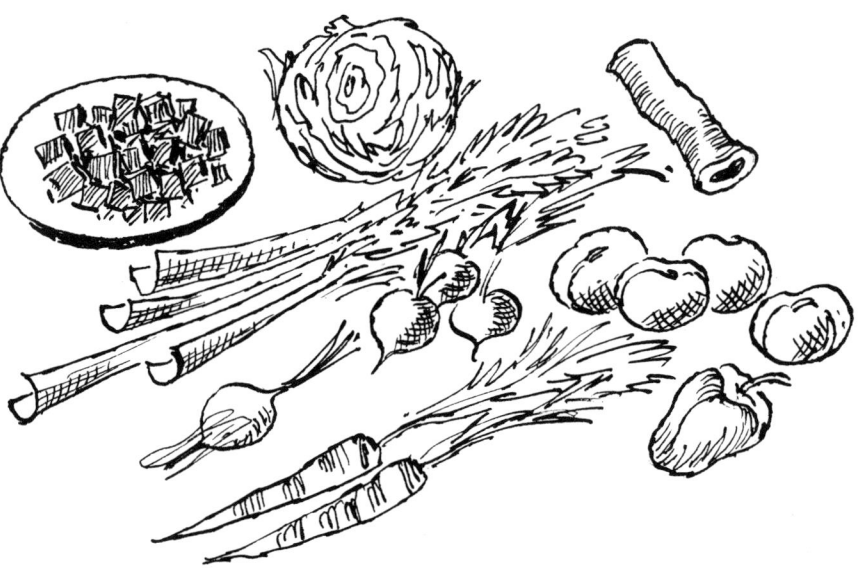

MY FAVORITE BORSTCH

2 pounds soup meat and bone	3 tomatoes, fresh or canned
2 to 3 sprigs parsley	1 cup carrots, diced
Sprig dill weed	5 fresh beets
1 bay leaf	3 potatoes, diced
1 small cabbage, shredded finely	1 green pepper, diced coarsely
1 onion, diced coarsely	Salt and pepper to taste

Put the meat, soup bone, parsley, dill weed and bay leaf in a large, deep pot, cover the meat with water and cook, covered, for 2 hours, or until the meat is very tender. Remove the soup bone and the parsley, dill weed and bay leaf. Add the cabbage, onion, tomatoes and carrots to the stock and meat and let simmer for 30 minutes.

Meanwhile, wash the beets and boil them separately for about 30 minutes, or until they are tender. Then peel and either slice or dice them coarsely. Set aside the water in which the beets were cooked.

Add the potatoes and green pepper to the vegetable stock mixture and cook for another 25 minutes. Add the beets and the water in which they were cooked, simmer an additional 10 minutes and serve. Pass the sour cream in a separate dish and stir a heaping spoonful into each dish of soup.   *Serves 8*

UKRAINIAN BORSTCHOK

2 bunches beets	¼ cup vinegar
8 cups beef bouillon or stock	½ pound frankfurters, diced

Wash, peel and thinly slice the beets. Put them in a deep pot, cover with the stock and vinegar and boil, covered, until the beets are tender, or about 30 minutes. Add the frankfurters and let simmer for an additional 5 minutes. Serve with sour cream passed in a separate bowl and stirred into the individual dishes of soup. *Serves 4*

GREEN STCHEE
(Cream of Spinach Soup)

1½ pounds soup meat	Salt and pepper to taste
8 cups water	1 cup sour cream
2 pounds fresh spinach	1 tablespoon flour
1½ tablespoons butter	2 hard boiled eggs

Put the soup meat in a deep pot, cover with water and cook, covered, for about 1 hour. Strain, reserve the stock, and keep the meat aside to use later for another purpose. (You may substitute 8 cups of beef bouillon, either canned or made from bouillon cubes, for the meat stock if you wish.)

Cook the spinach in a little water until it is tender. Put it in the empty soup pot, add the butter and sour cream, salt and pepper to taste, and let it cook over a very low heat for about 5 minutes — the spinach should have enough liquid left in it so it will not scorch. Add the stock (or bouillon) to the spinach mixture, thicken with a tablespoon or so of flour mixed with water to a smooth paste, and bring to a boil. At serving time, cut the hard boiled eggs into quarters and put them in the soup or slice and float on top. *Serves 4 to 6*

POTATO SOUP

6 large potatoes	2 small onions, diced
Fresh parsley, chopped	6 tablespoons bacon drippings
6 tablespoons butter	Salt and pepper to taste

Pare the potatoes and cut them into small pieces. Put them and the parsley in a deep pot, cover with water and start over a low fire. In a frying pan, melt the butter, add the onions and sauté until light brown and translucent. When the water in which the potatoes are cooking begins to boil, add the onions, cover and turn down the heat, letting the soup simmer. Meanwhile, put the bacon drippings into the frying pan the onions cooked in and, when melted, add enough flour to make a smooth paste. Let the mixture brown, but be sure it doesn't burn. Stir the paste into the soup and cook until the potatoes are soft, or about 1 hour. *Serves 6*

CABBAGE SOUP

1½ pounds soup meat

10 cups water

1 No. 2 can tomatoes

1 large onion, chopped coarsely

1 clove garlic, minced

1 bay leaf

Salt and pepper to taste

1 medium head cabbage

1 tablespoon vinegar

2 tablespoons sugar

Place the meat and water in a deep pot, add the tomatoes, onion, garlic and bay leaf. Salt and pepper to taste. Cover and simmer gently for 2 hours. Shred the cabbage coarsely and add it to the soup mixture, along with the vinegar and sugar. Simmer for another 1½ hours. Add more salt if needed. *Serves 6 to 8*

STCHEE
(Sauerkraut Soup)

2 pounds fresh or canned
  sauerkraut
1 onion, chopped
2 tablespoons butter

8 to 10 cups beef bouillon or
  stock made from leftover meat
5 potatoes, diced
Salt and pepper to taste

Wash the sauerkraut thoroughly, cover with cold water and bring to a boil. Then strain it and again rinse in cold water. Chop it and put into a deep pot. In a separate pan, brown the onion in the butter, then add it and the stock to the sauerkraut, and cook over a low fire for 1 hour. Add the potatoes and cook until they are done. Season to taste. Serve with individual side dishes of buttered buckwheat *kasha*. Also pass sour cream to be spooned into the soup, if desired.

Serves 6 to 8

SAUERKRAUT SOUP II

1 onion, chopped
2 tablespoons butter
1 tablespoon flour
1 pound fresh or canned
  sauerkraut

1 tablespoon tomato pureé
8 cups beef bouillon or
  meat stock
½ cup sour cream

Brown the onion in the butter. Stir in the flour, tomato paste and sauerkraut. Simmer for 10 minutes. Add the bouillon and cook for 30 minutes, or until the flavors are well blended. Stir in the sour cream.

Serves 6

RASSOLNIK
(Kidney Soup)

1 veal or beef kidney	3 potatoes
8 cups bouillon (including	3 dill pickles, peeled
kidney stock)	½ cup pickle juice
2 carrots	1 tablespoon flour
1 stalk celery	1 teaspoon butter
1 onion	Salt and pepper
1 bay leaf	

Place the kidney in a pan of cold water and bring to a boil. Drain, again cover it with cold water and bring to a boil. Repeat this process twice more to remove the strong flavor. Then again cover the kidney with cold water and cook until tender, approximately 20 minutes. Reserve the final water in which it was cooked and add it to the bouillon to make 8 cups of liquid. Slice the kidney and set it aside.

Peel and dice the vegetables, including the pickles, and put them in a deep pot with the pickle juice and stock. Cook for about 30 minutes, or until tender. Add the kidney. Let the mixture simmer for a few minutes, then thicken the soup with the flour which has been mixed to a paste with water. Add the butter and let the mixture come to a boil. Serve with sour cream spooned into the individual portions.

Serves 6

COD SOUP

1½ cups soup greens (including parsley, celery leaves, etc.)
2 bay leaves
10 cups water
3 pounds cod filets

1 small head cauliflower
12 to 16 ounces asparagus tips
3 slices lemon
Salt and pepper

Place the soup greens and the bay leaves in a deep pot, add the water and let cook, covered, for 30 minutes to make a stock. Strain. Slice the fish and cook it in the stock until tender. Cook the cauliflower and the asparagus separately and cut them into pieces. Add these and the lemon slices to the soup just before serving. *Serves 6 to 8*

SHRIMP SOUP

3 dozen average raw shrimp, cleaned
1½ cups soup greens (parsley, celery leaves, etc.)
1 onion, chopped
½ cup uncooked rice

1 tablespoon flour
1½ tablespoons vegetable oil
Salt and pepper to taste
1 cup sour cream
Parsley for garnish

Place the shrimp in a deep pot, add the soup greens and onion, cover with water and cook for 20 minutes with the pot covered. Strain and return the stock to the pan. Cook the rice separately and reserve. Peel the shrimp and dice them. Return to the stock, with the cooked rice. Thicken the soup with the flour, which has been browned in the vegetable oil. Add the sour cream; garnish with parsley and serve.

Serves 6

MUSHROOM SOUP

½ pound fresh mushrooms   2 onions

1 cup barley   1 tablespoon butter

5 potatoes, peeled and diced   ½ tablespoon flour

8 to 10 cups beef bouillon   Salt and pepper to taste

Dice the mushrooms and sauté in butter for 5 minutes. Boil the barley separately. Place the mushrooms and barley in a large, deep pot, and cover with the potatoes and bouillon. Simmer for 30 minutes. Peel and chop the onions, brown them in butter, sprinkle the flour over them and when it is blended in and brown, add the mixture gradually to the soup. Stir in well and thicken. Add salt and pepper to taste.

Note: An even better flavor is given to this soup when you can find dried white mushrooms. Use one large package to equal the half pound of fresh mushrooms. Cook them according to the package directions, slice and fry them, and proceed with the rest of the recipe. Be sure to save the water in which they were cooked and use it, with the bouillon, to make the 8 to 10 cups of liquid required.

Serves 6 to 8

MAIN COURSES
— So Much to Choose from

Selecting a main course to serve at a Russian dinner can be a tantalizing experience. There is so much to choose from! Each variety of meat, poultry or fish may be prepared in many different ways, all of them delicious. Then there are the vegetable dishes used during Lent as whole meals in themselves.

It is difficult but not impossible to plan a simple Russian dinner menu. The number of guests you intend to serve has a great deal to do with the final selections. The more people, the more dishes you can prepare without overwhelming your friends with the quantity of food offered. But you do not necessarily have to double each recipe if you are having twelve people for dinner and the recipe serves six. By the time you have served *zakuski,* perhaps a soup with *piroshki,* and have side dishes of salad and vegetables, the main course will stretch, believe me!

Thus it is best to follow one of two choices. Either serve a simple meat, chicken or fish dish and go heavily Russian on the vegetables that accompany it, or else have a very Russian main dish and settle for buttered vegetables and a tossed salad for accompaniments. Either would be perfectly correct. Doing it this way will not only make preparing the meal a pleasure instead of a chore, but will also serve as a better initiation for your guests. Many of the Russian vegetable dishes are quite rich. To combine them with a rich meat dish, particularly after the other preliminaries, would make too heavy a meal for most Americans.

BEEF STROGANOV

1½ pounds round steak	1 tablespoon tomato paste
2 tablespoons butter	2 cups beef bouillon
½ pound mushrooms, sliced	3 tablespoons sour cream
1 tablespoon onion, chopped	Salt and pepper to taste
1 tablespoon flour	

Slice the round steak in long, thin strips, cutting slightly on the diagonal and across the grain of the meat. By cutting across rather than with the grain your pieces will be more tender in the end — almost the equivalent of a boneless sirloin (which can also be used in this recipe, but is much more expensive).

Melt the butter in a large skillet and sauté the mushrooms and onions until the latter are golden and transparent. Remove them from the skillet and set aside. Put the meat slices in the skillet, salt them, and then sear very quickly, turning once. Add the mushrooms and onions. Add the flour, and toss until the meat is coated. Then add the tomato paste, bouillon and sour cream. Mix well and let simmer for about 5 minutes. Although rice, mashed potatoes or egg noodles may be served with this, the real Russian way is to serve *stroganov* with fried potatoes. (Frozen shoestring potatoes are perfect; just fry them in a little hot oil, then sprinkle with salt.)   *Serves 6*

BEEF AND MUSHROOM CASSEROLE

1½ pounds round steak
3 tablespoons butter
 plus extra for frying
2 onions, finely sliced

½ pound mushrooms, sliced
1 tablespoon flour
2 cups sour cream
Salt and pepper to taste

Cut the meat into small chunks, about 2 inches thick, then flatten the pieces with a cleaver. Salt and pepper the meat, then sear it in butter until browned. Sauté the onions and the mushrooms separately until they begin to brown. Butter a 2-quart casserole, place a layer of meat on the bottom, then a layer of mushrooms and onions, another of meat and so on. The top layer should be of meat. Melt 3 tablespoons of butter, mix the flour into it and stir in the sour cream. Pour this sauce over the casserole. Bake, covered, at 375°F for 30 minutes, or until the meat is tender. Potatoes, *kasha* or noodles go well with this dish.

Serves 6

BEEF SOUFFLÉ

2 onions, chopped
1 cup bread crumbs
½ cup hot milk
1 tablespoon butter

1½ cups ground round steak
1 cup boiled cabbage, chopped
2 eggs
Salt and pepper to taste

Sauté the onions in a little butter until golden brown. Mix together the onions, bread crumbs, hot milk, butter, ground round steak and boiled cabbage. Separate the eggs, beat the yolks and fold them into the meat mixture. Add salt and pepper to taste. Whip the whites until stiff and gently fold them into the meat mixture. Turn into a greased 2-quart casserole or soufflé dish and bake at 375°F for 30 minutes.

Serves 6

PASHTET OF BEEF

5 hard rolls
1 cup milk
2 pounds round steak
5 potatoes
½ cup bread crumbs
2 onions, sliced thinly

½ teaspoon ground cloves
3 eggs
½ cup grated Swiss or American
cheese
Salt and pepper to taste

Set the rolls aside to soak in enough milk to cover them while preparing the other ingredients. Slice the round steak into thin strips, cut across the grain, and set aside. Boil the potatoes, cool and peel them, and cut into fairly thin slices. Butter a 2-quart casserole. Sprinkle the bottom with dry bread crumbs, then add a layer of onions and a layer of meat, and season with salt, pepper and cloves. Add another layer of onions and a layer of potatoes. Salt and pepper and dot with butter. Repeat until all the ingredients are used. Beat the eggs, then mash the milk-soaked rolls and add them, with the milk in which they have been soaked, to the beaten eggs. Pour over the casserole contents, sprinkle with bread crumbs and grated cheese, and bake at 375°F for about 30 minutes, or until brown.

Serves 6 to 8

BEEF CUTLETS

2 pounds lean, boneless beef	1 onion, chopped
¼ pound suet	Butter for frying
7 slices bread	Bread crumbs for coating
½ cup water	Salt and pepper to taste

Ask your butcher to put the beef and the suet through his grinder twice. This should be a very fine mixture. Soak the bread in just enough water to saturate it and when it is thoroughly wet, squeeze it out and mix the bread and meat together. Brown the onion in butter, then add it to the meat-bread mixture. Salt and pepper to taste. If the mixture seems too stiff to handle, add a little water. Form into 12 balls. Roll each of the balls in bread crumbs, then form into a flat oblong shape like a cutlet. Brown these well on each side in butter over a high heat. Reduce the heat and cook until they are done; about 15 minutes. Pass sour cream in a separate dish to be served with the cutlets. *Serves 6*

GOLUBTSI
(Cabbage Rolls)

1 cabbage	Salt and pepper
1 pound ground round steak or chuck	1 small onion, chopped
	1 egg
¼ pound ground pork	Cooking oil for frying
¼ cup boiled rice	3 tablespoons butter
1 teaspoon chopped parsley or ½ teaspoon dill weed	2 tablespoons flour
	2 cups tomato soup
1 cup mushrooms, chopped (optional)	¼ teaspoon sugar
	1 cup sour cream

Parboil the cabbage for about 5 minutes, remove from the water and let cool. Separate 12 large leaves from the cabbage head and trim the hard part away from the bases of the leaves. Wrap the balance of the cabbage in foil and store in the refrigerator for future use (there are many other Russian recipes you may use it in or, since it will not be cooked through in that length of time, you can make cole slaw with it).

Mix the chopped meats with the boiled rice, chopped parsley, salt, pepper and mushrooms. Sauté the onion slightly and add it. Add the egg and stir the mixture well. Put one generous tablespoon of meat in the middle of each cabbage leaf and then roll it lengthwise, tucking in the edges so that the finished product is like a stuffed envelope. Heat enough vegetable oil to cover the bottom of the frying pan and sauté the cabbage rolls, carefully putting them in seam side down and later turning them over, until they are delicately brown. Lightly oil a large, flat casserole and arrange the cabbage rolls on the bottom of it as you finish cooking them. Keep adding oil to the frying pan as needed so that it is well greased at all times.

Melt 3 tablespoons of butter in a clean frying pan, add the flour and then slowly add the tomato soup and sugar. Simmer this sauce until it is slightly thickened. Cover the cabbage rolls with the sauce and bake, covered, for 30 minutes at 350°F. Remove from the oven, spread sour cream over the top and return to the oven for about 10 minutes, or until the top is bubbling.   *Serves 6*

PELMENY
(Russian Ravioli)

Dough

2 cups flour (approx.)	¾ teaspoon salt
2 eggs	½ cup water

Filling

1½ pounds ground beef	Salt and pepper to taste
2 onions, finely chopped	Enough water to make the filling juicy

One of the most popular traditional dishes in San Francisco is *pelmeny,* the Russian version of ravioli. They can be purchased frozen in Russian groceries and delicatessens, and one church group has made quite a successful fund-raising enterprise by making *pelmeny,* freezing them and then supplying them to homes. While in San Francisco recently, I woke up one morning to hear much Russian conversation going on out in the hallway. When I asked my hostess who the early visitor had been, she said, "The *pelmeny* man. He comes once a month."

For the dough, mix the flour, eggs and salt with the water into a firm paste and let stand for 1 hour. (The precise amount of flour needed to make the mixture stiff enough to handle must be gauged by the individual.) Roll the dough out so that it is very thin, and then cut it into circles about 2½ inches in diameter.

For the filling, mix the meat, onion, salt and pepper together, add enough water to make the filling juicy, and put a small mound of the mixture in the center of each round of dough. With your finger, smooth a little cold water along the edge of one half of the circle. Fold over and press the two edges together, then crimp them firmly. It is important that they be very firmly sealed. You may use them in this shape but, to be absolutely correct, there is one more step. The ends of the turnovers are brought together and pinched firmly, to form a ball. Carefully lower the *pelmeny* into boiling water (in which you may dissolve a couple of chicken bouillon cubes for added flavor). Cook for 15 minutes. Remove carefully and drain. These are best served with soy sauce, sour cream and/or vinegar. *Serves 4 to 6*

Note: An acceptable substitute for the real Russian *pelmeny* can be made by purchasing frozen, meat-filled Italian ravioli available in almost any grocery store. Cook according to the package directions and serve with sour cream and soy sauce. Also put a flacon of vinegar on the table, to be used as desired; this is the Siberian way of eating *pelmeny*.

CAUCASIAN SHASHLIK

2 pounds lamb

1 onion, sliced

1 pint vinegar

2 tablespoons salt

2 bay leaves

3 whole cloves

½ teaspoon nutmeg or cinnamon

2 cloves garlic, minced

Salt and pepper to taste

1 pint water

1 sprig parsley

1 pound bacon

Cut the lamb into large bite-sized chunks suitable for threading on skewers. Flatten each piece with a wooden mallet and salt and pepper to taste. Set aside. Put all the other ingredients except the bacon into a deep pot for a marinade, bring to a boil and let simmer for 5 minutes. Cool slightly. Put the meat in a large bowl, pour the warm marinade over it and mix thoroughly. Let it stand for several hours or overnight. Remove the meat and drain on paper towels. Thread it on skewers, putting a square of bacon between each piece of meat. Broil in the oven or over a barbecue for about 10 minutes, turning occasionally. Serve with plain boiled rice. This is a first cousin to shish kebab, but has quite a different flavor.   *Serves 4 to 6*

PILAV OF LAMB

3 pounds lamb shoulder,
with bone
1 large onion, chopped

2 tablespoons butter
1 cup uncooked rice
Salt and pepper to taste

Cut the meat off the bones into bite-sized chunks and fry in butter, with the onion, until nicely browned. Salt and pepper to taste and set aside. Cover the lamb bones with about 5 cups of water and cook for 20 minutes. Put the meat-onion mixture in a fairly deep pot, add the rice and stir. Then add 4 cups of the lamb stock, cover and cook over a slow fire for about 20 minutes, or until the rice is done.

Serves 6 to 8

BILISHI
(Russian Hamburgers)

1 package hot roll mix

1 pound ground lamb (lean beef
  may be substituted)

1 onion, chopped

1 clove garlic, chopped

Salt and pepper to taste

Vegetable oil as needed

Follow the package directions for making basic dough, but use ¾ cup water and 1 egg in place of 1 cup of water. Let the dough rise, according to the directions. Meanwhile, make a filling by mixing together the ground meat, onion, garlic, salt and pepper. Add a few teaspoons of cold water to make the mixture soft and juicy.

When the dough has doubled in bulk, punch it down and roll it out about ¼-inch thick. Cut into circles with a large biscuit cutter (about 2½ to 3 inches in diameter). Put a liberal tablespoon of meat filling in the center of each round and spread it almost to the edges. Now crimp the edges so that they just cover the edge of the meat mixture. You will have a flat, open-faced meat tart when you are finished, with the dough edges tucked over the meat.

Heat just enough oil to cover the bottom of a frying pan and carefully slip the tarts into the pan, meat side down. You will be able to cook from 3 to 5 of them at a time, depending upon the size of your frying pan. Cook for approximately 5 minutes, then turn them with a spatula and cook about 5 minutes on the other side. They should be a deep golden brown on top when finished. Add additional oil as needed. Serve hot or cold, with soy sauce. This, I am told, is a Tartar dish that goes way back in Russian history. *Yields 24 bilishi*

VEAL WITH CHERRIES

4 pounds veal roast

25 to 30 sour cherries, pitted
(fresh or canned)

2 tablespoons melted butter

2 teaspoons cardamon

½ teaspoon cinnamon

2 tablespoons flour

½ cup cherry juice,
fresh or canned

½ cup dry white wine

1 cup chicken bouillon

Salt and pepper to taste

First rub the veal roast with salt and pepper. Then, with a sharp knife, make incisions on the surface and insert one of the cherries into each cut. If fresh cherries are not available, canned pie cherries are acceptable. Use about 25 to 30 cherries in all. Place the veal on a roasting pan and brush it with the melted butter. Sprinkle it with cardamon and cinnamon. Quickly brown it over a high fire. Sprinkle it with the flour, cover the roaster and cook in a 350°F degree oven for 30 minutes. Mix the cherry juice with the wine and bouillon, pour it over the roast, again cover and cook for about 1½ hours, basting occasionally, until the veal is well done. To serve, slice the meat and arrange it on a platter. Heat the pan sauce, pour it over the meat and garnish with additional cherries, if desired. *Serves 8*

VEAL KIDNEYS IN MADEIRA

4 or 5 veal kidneys	1½ tablespoons flour
Salt and pepper to taste	2 cups chicken bouillon
3 tablespoons butter	1 liqueur glass of Madeira

Wash the kidneys and soak them in water for an hour or so. Dry, pare and cut them into slices. Salt and pepper to taste. Sauté the kidneys in 2 tablespoons of butter over a hot fire for about 10 minutes, stirring them frequently so that they will not scorch. Make a sauce by mixing 1 melted tablespoon of butter with the flour, then stir constantly as the bouillon and Madeira are gradually added. Pour the sauce over the kidneys, cover and let simmer for 20 minutes.

Serves 4 to 6

MOSCOW SPECIAL

2 pounds fresh or canned
   sauerkraut
¼ pound butter
½ tablespoon flour
2 onions, finely chopped
1½ cups bouillon

1 to 2 cups cooked veal,
   chicken or ham, diced
8 to 10 olives
1 dill pickle
6 or 8 pickled mushrooms

Drain and rinse the sauerkraut. Melt the butter and blend in the flour, onion and bouillon. Cover and simmer until thoroughly mixed, about 10 minutes. Grease a 1½-quart casserole. Place half the sauerkraut mixture in it, top with the cooked meat and cover with sauerkraut. Slice the dill pickle, olives and mushrooms and decorate the top. Bake until brown at 350°F for about 1 hour. *Serves 6 to 8*

PIROG

Dough

3 packages active dry yeast	6 egg yolks
2 cups warm milk	1 teaspoon salt
4 cups flour	2 tablespoons sugar
½ pound sweet butter, softened	1 beaten egg yolk

Dissolve the yeast in ½ cup warm milk and set aside. Mix the flour and softened butter in a large bowl, add the remaining ingredients except the beaten egg yolk, and add the yeast mixture last. Beat until the ingredients are thoroughly mixed, then set aside in a warm place to rise for about 1 hour, or until the dough has doubled in size.

Divide the dough into two equal parts and knead each lightly on a floured board. Roll each piece out to fit a baking pan 9 x 12 inches in size. Grease the pan with butter and put one piece of the dough in it, spreading it to the edges. Add one of the fillings listed below, then top with the second part of the dough, rolled out so that it will cover the filling. Pinch the edges together with a fork, pierce the top of the pie, then brush it with the beaten egg yolk and bake at 350°F for 30 minutes, or until nicely browned.

Note: This dough recipe may also be used if you wish to make *piroshki* dough from scratch. *Pirog*, incidentally, is the traditional Russian birthday cake.

Meat filling

2 pounds ground round steak	Salt and pepper to taste
1 onion, chopped	¼ cup beef bouillon
1 tablespoon butter	1 egg yolk, beaten
4 hard boiled eggs, chopped	

Fry the ground round and the onion in butter. When browned, cool, then add the hard boiled eggs. Salt and pepper to taste, add the bouillon and mix well together. Fill the *pirog* shell with the meat mixture, cover with the rolled top dough. Pinch the sides together firmly. Make a little opening in the center with a knife to let the steam escape, brush the top with the beaten egg yolk and then bake.

Fish filling

1 pound white fish filets
1 onion, chopped
2 tablespoons butter

1 cup cooked rice
1 hard boiled egg, chopped
Salt and pepper to taste

Boil the fish for 20 minutes, or until it flakes. Cool, then cut it into small pieces. Sauté the onion in butter, mix with the fish, then add salt and pepper to taste. Add the rice, hard boiled egg, and fill the *pirog* shell. Top with the upper crust and bake as directed.

Rice and egg filling

1 cup cooked rice
2 hard boiled eggs, chopped
2 tablespoons butter

1 sprig parsley, chopped
Salt and pepper to taste

Mix the above ingredients, moisten with a little bouillon if necessary, fill the *pirog* shell and bake as directed. *All variations serve 12*

PUFF PASTE PIROG

1¾ cup flour

½ cup ice water

Salt to taste

½ pound cold butter

A delicious and festive *pirog* may be made by using puff paste. Mix the flour and water, salt to taste, and roll out on a floured board to a ½-inch thickness. Place ¼ of the butter in pieces on half of the dough, then bring the other half over it and pinch the edges together. Refrigerate for 1 hour. Again roll the dough out, dot it with ¼ of the butter, fold over the other half and refrigerate for approximately 1 hour. Repeat this process until all the butter has been used. Let the dough chill thoroughly and then proceed as with regular *pirog*.

CHICKEN KIEV

3 boned chicken breasts

1 cup unsalted butter,
   well chilled

Bread crumbs for coating

Salt and pepper to taste

1 egg

Parsley for garnish

Split the chicken breasts, allowing one half breast per serving. Pound the chicken very thin. Knead the butter into little rolls about 2 inches long and ½ inch thick. Chill these thoroughly — it is a good idea to put them in the freezer for a couple of hours. Place 1 butter roll in the center of each chicken breast half, roll the chicken over and around it, and then fasten it firmly with toothpicks. The idea is to surround the butter completely with the chicken meat so that none will leak out in the cooking process. Season the bread crumbs to taste with salt and pepper. Beat the egg in a little cold water. Dip the chicken rolls in the bread crumbs, then in the egg and then roll in bread crumbs again. Fry in deep fat (either lard or vegetable oil) until golden brown. Drain and keep warm in the oven until ready to serve. Each roll should be served atop a slice of toast and garnished with parsley. This is one of the internationally famous Russian dishes — very delicious, but rich. Keep the vegetables and other accompaniments simple when serving it.

Serves 6

CHICKEN KIEV WITH MUSHROOMS

2 tablespoons mushrooms,
   finely chopped

1 teaspoon onion, grated

1 teaspoon parsley,
   finely minced

Follow the basic recipe for Chicken Kiev, but add the above ingredients to the chilled butter.

GALANTINE OF CHICKEN

1 roasting chicken	½ pound mushrooms
1 pound veal	1 tablespoon butter
½ pound pork	Salt and pepper to taste

Cut the chicken meat away from the bones and put it through a meat grinder with the veal and pork, mushrooms, butter and salt and pepper to taste. Turn it into a well-greased mold — if you don't have a pudding mold with a lid use a 2-pound coffee can — cover, put in a large pot, cover with water and boil for 2 hours. Chill thoroughly and serve sliced. *Serves 6 to 8*

TURKEY WITH WALNUT SAUCE

4 slices white bread, crusts removed	1 teaspoon salt
1 cup chicken bouillon	Dash cayenne pepper
2 tablespoons butter	16 slices leftover turkey
½ cup onion, chopped	8 slices toast
2 cups walnuts, ground or finely chopped	

Soak the bread in the bouillon until it is thoroughly saturated, remove and mash until smooth. Melt the butter in a frying pan and sauté the onions until they are golden. Mash them and add to the mashed bread, along with the walnuts, salt and pepper. The sauce should be about the consistency of hollandaise or mayonnaise; if too thick, add a little more bouillon. Arrange the turkey slices on toast and cover with the sauce. *Serves 8*

CHRISTMAS GOOSE

8-pound goose   ¼ pound unsalted butter
Caraway seeds   1 tablespoon vinegar
Pepper   Salt and pepper to taste
1 medium red cabbage

Rub the outside of the goose with pepper and caraway seeds. Set
aside. Shred the cabbage, then heat the butter in a large skillet and
add the cabbage, vinegar, salt and pepper. Simmer for 10 minutes,
stirring so it will not scorch. Cool. Stuff the cavity of the goose with
the cabbage mixture and roast at 300°F for 30 minutes to the pound,
or until the goose is very well done. Occasionally prick the skin with
a sharp-tined fork to allow the grease to run out. This is very good
served with mashed potatoes and applesauce, or with oven-roasted
potatoes. A gravy may be made from the pan drippings, but it makes
very rich fare.   *Serves 4 to 6*

PLUM SAUCE

1 pound fresh plums, pitted   1 tablespoon parsley, minced
3 cloves garlic, minced   Salt and pepper to taste

Put the plums in a saucepan, cover them with water and cook, covered,
for about 30 minutes, or until they are tender. Drain, reserving the
liquid. Put the plums through a sieve or pureé them in a blender.
Add the garlic, parsley, salt and pepper. Add enough plum liquid
to give the mixture the consistency of thick cream. Bring it to a boil,
reduce the heat and simmer for 5 minutes. This may be served either
hot or cold, and is very good with *shashlik*, roast chicken or other fowl.

STUFFED FISH

3-pound whole fish   2 tablespoons flour

1 pound sauerkraut   5 tablespoons butter

1 onion   Salt and pepper to taste

3 apples, peeled and diced

Clean and wash the fish and rub it with salt. Set aside. Cover the sauerkraut with cold water and bring to a boil. Change the water and repeat. Drain and let cold water run through the sauerkraut for a few minutes, then repeat the process again and let cook for 15 minutes. Meanwhile, chop the onion and sauté it in some of the butter. Drain the sauerkraut and add the onion, apples and half the remaining butter to it. Stuff the fish with this mixture and either sew it up or fasten it with pins. Sprinkle with flour. Brown in the rest of the butter and then bake it in a shallow greased dish at 375°F for 30 minutes, basting occasionally with the pan juices. *Serves 6*

COD WITH CHERRY SAUCE

2 pounds fresh cod filets

2 cups milk

Boiling water

1 cup sour cherries
  (canned), pitted

1⅔ cups water

2 tablespoons butter

1 tablespoon sugar
  (approximately)

¼ teaspoon cinnamon

¼ teaspoon cloves

1 cup red wine

1 tablespoon cornstarch

Wash the filets and cut them into serving-size slices. Put them in a sauce-pan, cover with milk and bring to a boil. Lower the heat and let simmer for 10 minutes. Drain and pour boiling water over the fish to rinse off all traces of the milk. Set aside.

Simmer the cherries, water and butter for 5 minutes, then add the sugar, cinnamon, cloves and the red wine (this should be a tart sauce). Simmer for 5 more minutes. Mix the cornstarch with a little cold water to make a thin paste and add it to the sauce, stirring constantly until it is thickened and shiny. Put the cooked fish into the sauce, cover and simmer over low heat for 10 more minutes. Serve with boiled rice or mashed potatoes. *Serves 4 to 6*

BOILED TROUT

3 pounds of trout
1 stalk celery, diced
1 bunch parsley

1 carrot, cut in strips
2 onions, sliced
Salt and pepper

Several hours before you plan to serve dinner, clean the fish and put in a deep pot. Make a stock by boiling all the vegetables together in water to cover for about 20 minutes. Let the stock cool. Cover the fish with it and set aside until about 1 hour before dinner. Bring the fish and stock to a boil over a high fire, then lower the heat and let simmer for about 20 minutes, or until tender. Before serving, remove the skin from the fish, arrange it on a heated platter, cover with melted butter and sprinkle with parsley. Serve with boiled potatoes. *Serves 4 to 6*

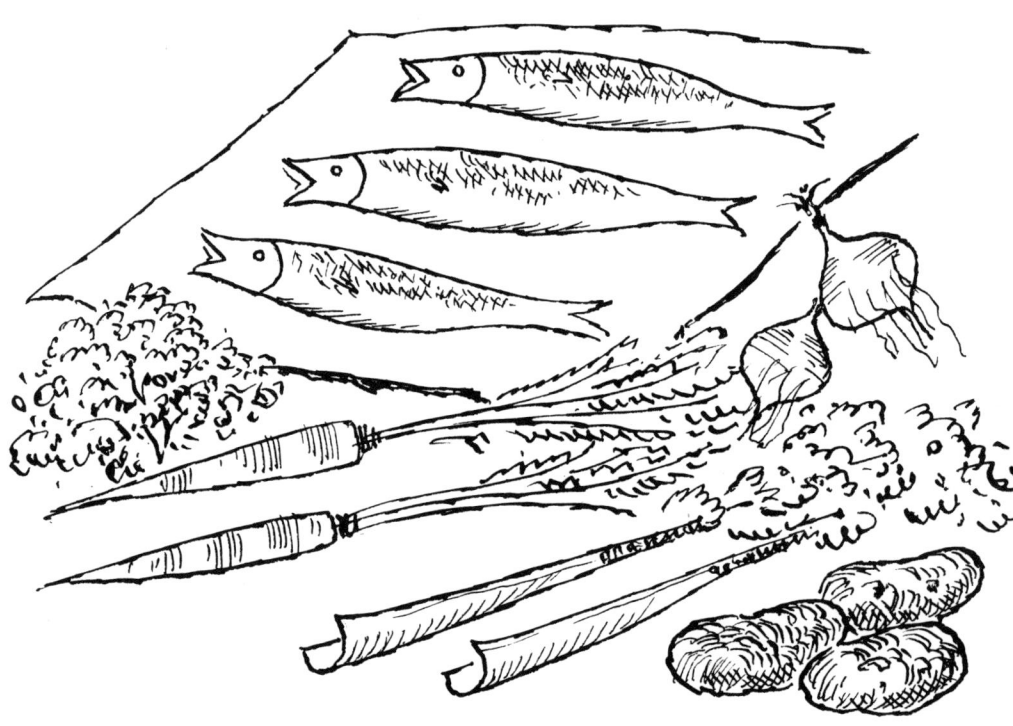

FISH FILETS IN SOUR CREAM

3 pounds fish filets

4 tablespoons flour

4 tablespoons butter

½ cup beef or chicken bouillon

1 cup sour cream

parsley for garnish

Salt and pepper to taste

Cut the filets into individual portions and season with salt and pepper. Roll in 3 tablespoons flour and fry in 3 tablespoons butter. When brown, remove from the frying pan and transfer to a lightly oiled baking dish. Cut the remaining tablespoon of butter into the remaining tablespoon of flour and add to the pan the fish has been cooked in. Gradually add the bouillon. Then stir in the sour cream and cook for several minutes to let the sauce thicken. Pour the sauce over the fish and bake, uncovered, at 450°F for 10 minutes. Garnish with parsley.

Serves 4 to 6

SALMON CASSEROLE

6 to 8 potatoes, thinly sliced	2 eggs
1 large onion, chopped	1 quart milk
½ pound smoked salmon	Salt and pepper to taste

Butter a 2-quart casserole and line the bottom with thinly sliced potatoes. Over this, sprinkle the onion and small strips of the smoked salmon. Repeat in layers until the dish is ¾ full. Beat the eggs and gradually add the milk to them. Add salt and pepper to taste and pour over the contents of the casserole. Add more milk if necessary to cover the potato mixture. Bake at 300°F for about 1½ hours, or until nicely browned.

Serves 4 to 6

CODFISH CASSEROLE

1 pound cod filets	1 large onion, sliced
(or any white fish filets)	½ pound fresh mushrooms
Flour for dusting	2 dill pickles, sliced lengthwise
Vegetable oil for frying	Salt and pepper to taste

Sprinkle the filets with salt and pepper and roll in flour. Fry in vegetable oil until lightly browned. Then place the fish in a lightly oiled baking dish. Sauté the onion in the same pan as the fish, and when it begins to become translucent, add the mushrooms and cook until they are tender. Add the dill pickles, mix together, sprinkle on top of the fish and bake, uncovered, at 375°F for 25 minutes.

Serves 4

KASHA

2 cups buckwheat grain
1 egg

2 tablespoons butter
Dash of salt

Mix the grain well with the egg. Place in a deep frying pan and stir over low heat until each grain is coated and separated. Then cover with boiling water, add the butter and the salt. Cook, covered, for about ½ hour. You may need to add a little more water from time to time to prevent the grains from scorching. Continue simmering until the grains are thoroughly cooked. Serve in individual bowls, with sour cream to taste. Pack any leftover *kasha* into a greased bread tin to be sliced and fried in butter later. It is delicious this way. Alternate methods of cooking the *kasha* may also be found on the package and are just as good.   *Serves 6 to 8*

KASHA AND MUSHROOMS

1 recipe kasha, as above
½ pound mushrooms, sliced
1 tablespoon onion, minced

2 tablespoons butter
Salt and pepper to taste

Prepare *kasha* according to the previous recipe or the package instructions. Sauté the mushrooms and onion in butter until the onion is translucent. Salt and pepper to taste and add to the cooked *kasha*. Also serve with sour cream passed at the table.   *Serves 6 to 8*

BANDURYANIK
(Potato Pudding)

3 large potatoes	½ cup sour cream
1 large onion	1 cup flour
2 eggs	Salt and pepper to taste

This is a favorite during Lent. Grate the potatoes and onion, or put them through a food grinder. Separate the eggs and beat the yolks. Add the sour cream and egg yolks, then gradually stir in the flour. Salt and pepper to taste. Beat the egg whites until stiff and fold in. Turn this mixture into a 9-inch greased pie plate (I prefer a glass one) and bake at 350°F for 30 minutes, or until the edges are nicely browned. *Serves 4 to 6*

POTATOES STUFFED WITH MUSHROOMS

6 large potatoes	Salt and pepper to taste
1 large or 2 small onions	½ pound mushrooms, chopped
1 egg, beaten	Melted butter and
2 tablespoons butter	Grated cheese for garnish
½ cup medium cream	

Parboil the potatoes for about 10 to 15 minutes, or until they are half done. Cool. Meanwhile, chop the onions and fry them in a little butter until they are tender. Peel the potatoes, then scoop out the center of each one and mash it thoroughly. Add the beaten egg, butter, cream, salt and pepper to taste, and the mushrooms. Spoon the stuffing into the potatoes and place in a baking dish. Pour a little melted butter over each potato, sprinkle with grated cheese and bake at 375°F for 20 minutes, or until browned. *Serves 6*

MOORSOFKA
(Lenten Vegetable Casserole)
**Approximately 1½ cups of each of the following, cut in
    fairly large chunks:**

Carrots	Onions
Parsnips	Zucchini
Green pepper	Eggplant
Celery	Tomatoes
½ to 1 cup parsley, chopped	1½ cups ketchup
1 clove garlic, chopped	Vegetable oil for frying

Have a 2-quart casserole ready. In a large skillet, start sautéing the above vegetables. Add oil as needed during the course of the cooking. Begin with the root vegetables — carrots, then parsnips, and move on to the celery, pepper, onions, zucchini, etc. Use quite a lot of onion and mix in the garlic as you cook it. Cook each vegetable until it is about half done (test with a fork) and transfer it to the casserole. When all the vegetables have been half cooked, stir them together in the casserole with the ketchup. Then bake, covered, in a 350°F oven for about 20 minutes, or until the carrots are fork tender. This may be served hot or cold. Usually it is served hot the first day as a Lenten supper, then the next day it is served cold.   *Serves 10 to 12*

BAKED EGGPLANT

1 large eggplant	2 cups milk
2 tablespoons butter	Salt and pepper to taste
1 tablespoon flour	2 tablespoons grated cheese

Peel the eggplant and cut it in half lengthwise. Remove the seeds. Cover the eggplant with water and boil until it is fork tender. Drain and place the two halves side by side in a buttered baking dish. Salt and pepper to taste.

Make a sauce by melting the butter, adding the flour to make a paste, and then gradually adding the milk. Pour the sauce over the eggplant, sprinkle with grated cheese and bake at 375°F for about 25 minutes, or until browned. *Serves 4 to 6*

STUFFED TURNIPS

6 small round turnips, yellow or white	2 cups milk
½ cup farina or cream of rice	2 tablespoons butter
	Salt and pepper to taste

Wash the turnips, then cover them with cold water and boil until fork tender, about 30 minutes. Let cool, then peel and slice off the tops. Set aside. Make a cooked cereal with the farina or cream of rice according to package directions, but using milk instead of water. Add salt and pepper to taste. Scoop out the centers of the turnips, mash them and add to the cereal. Add the butter. Stir the mixture well, then stuff the turnips with it. Cover each turnip with its top, put on a buttered cookie sheet, and bake in a 350°F oven for about 30 minutes, or until browned. *Serves 6*

STEWED CUCUMBERS

6 cucumbers	½ tablespoon flour
1 onion	2 cups chicken bouillon
1 tablespoon butter	1 cup sour cream

Peel the cucumbers, slice them thinly and sprinkle with salt. Put in a dish with a lid and cover them. Let them sit for ½ hour, then drain. Chop the onion and sauté it in butter. Add the drained cucumbers and cook until they are fork tender. Add the flour and stir thoroughly. Then gradually add the stock and sour cream, and bring to a boil. Serve with beef or lamb.

Serves 6

GREEN BEANS

1 onion, thinly sliced	1 3-ounce can sliced
1 tablespoon butter	mushrooms, drained
1 8-ounce can cut green	½ cup sour cream
beans, drained	Salt and pepper to taste

Sauté the onion in the butter until it is golden and translucent. Add the mushrooms and beans, and heat together. Mix in the sour cream. Salt and pepper to taste.

Serves 4

FROM PIROSHKI
TO BLACK BREAD

When I was a child and had dinner in a Russian restaurant or at the
home of Russian friends, *piroshki* fascinated me. They looked like
oval rolls — yet deep inside there was always a delicious filling, and
I could never quite figure out how it got there, for the surface always
seemed perfectly smooth, all the way around.

Piroshki should be smooth and oval, but it takes practice to have
them come out all that perfectly. It doesn't take practice, however, to
make a *piroshki* that, while not quite so eye-pleasing, will be just as
delicious. These little "stuffed rolls" are remarkable food. They are
to the Russians what hamburgers and hot dogs combined might be to

Americans; a versatile food, right for just about any occasion. Small *piroshki* may be served as a hot *zakuski*. Regular *piroshki,* about the size of oval French dinner rolls, are great for lunch, a perfect teatime snack, and taste good either hot or cold. When served with a soup course, bouillon is the best choice; a thick *borstch* or other hearty soup is really too filling.

There are quite a few *piroshki* take-out shops in San Francisco now, and I wish that they extended over considerably more of the country. For *piroshki* are among the world's best "finger foods."

Here again, convenience foods play a large role today. I was taught to make *piroshki* with hot roll mix. Some people fry *piroshki;* other Russian women bake theirs. I like them both ways, and it would be difficult to make a decision between them. The same thing goes for the fillings. Most traditional is the meat filling made with ground beef, but there are a number of others — all good.

Short cuts are perfectly permissible in the culinary arts today and, as I've said, Russian housewives in San Francisco regularly use convenience foods in their recipes — provided the quality does not suffer.

So during *Maslenitza* week, *bliny* — small Russian pancakes — are more often than not made with packaged pancake mix, especially the buckwheat variety, and there is nothing wrong with this. Simply follow the package directions and then use the traditional fish and sour cream toppings.

But to be totally traditional about it, *bliny* should be made with a raised yeast dough. For the fun of it, try the real thing sometime.

PIROSHKI I

Dough
1 package hot roll mix

Prepare and raise the hot roll mix according to the package directions, except use ¾ cup of water and 1 egg instead of the 1 cup of water given in the basic recipe. When the dough has doubled, punch it down and then knead it. Roll it out to a ½-inch thickness and cut it into 20 equal pieces with a sharp knife. Roll out each piece with a rolling pin until it is about the size of a large apple and then pull the dough into an elongated oval. Put a tablespoon or so of your selected filling (recipes for which follow) in the center of each round of dough. Then bring the ends together the long way and pinch them tight to form an oval. The more skillful you get, the smoother the dough will be over the filling, and the less your pinched seam will show after cooking. This takes just plain practice. It is important that this seam be a real seal, however, especially if you plan to fry the *piroshki.*

As you fill and seal the *piroshki,* put them on a platter which has first been covered with a towel and sprinkled with flour. Sprinkle the *piroshki* with flour and cover with another towel so that they won't dry out.

To fry, put about 3 inches of oil into a 2-quart saucepan. Let the oil heat through, then try it with a little bit of dough. When dropped in, it should quickly bob to the surface and brown. When the oil is ready, slip in the *piroshki,* pinched side down. This is so that the seam area will cook quickly and make the seal a secure one. Fry until brown, turn and fry on the other side — about 2 minutes to each side. Drain on paper towels. *Piroshki* may be frozen after cooking; reheat them in the oven before serving.

To bake *piroshki,* brush each one with egg yolk diluted with water. This will give them a golden brown, shiny finish. Put them seam side down on a cookie sheet, which has been lightly greased and floured, and bake at 400°F for 15 minutes. Then lower the heat to 350° and bake for 15 to 20 minutes more.

Meat filling

½ onion, chopped finely
Cooking oil for frying
1 pound lean ground beef

3 hard boiled eggs, chopped
Beef bouillon, for moisture

Heat about a tablespoon of oil in a frying pan and sauté the onions in it until they are translucent and golden brown. Add the meat and stir until it is slightly browned, then add the eggs and a little bouillon to moisten the mixture. Set aside to cool before using in the *piroshki*.

Potato filling

4 potatoes, peeled
1 egg
1 onion, finely chopped

2 tablespoons butter
¼ teaspoon nutmeg
Salt and pepper

Boil the potatoes until they are tender, then mash them (or use prepared mashed potatoes). Beat in the egg. Then add the onion, butter, nutmeg, salt and pepper. A little milk may be added for moisture, if desired. Fill the *piroshki* and proceed as above.

Fish filling

½ pound cooked or canned
   salmon
2 hard boiled eggs, chopped
2 cups cooked rice

5 to 6 mushrooms, chopped
   (optional)
Salt and pepper to taste

Canned red salmon is an excellent choice for this filling. Break the fish with a fork and blend in all the other ingredients. Moisten with a little bouillon, if desired.   *All variations yield 20 piroshki*

PIROSHKI II

1 cup warm milk	2 tablespoons sugar
1 yeast cake	3 cups flour
2 eggs	3 tablespoons melted butter

This is the "from scratch" method. Mix the warm milk, yeast, eggs and sugar in a large bowl. Gradually add the flour and mix thoroughly. Add the melted butter. Turn the dough out on a floured board and knead for 10 minutes. Return the dough to the bowl. Brush the top of the dough with oil, cover with a cloth and let rise in a warm place until doubled in bulk — 1 to 2 hours. Punch the dough down, turn it out onto a lightly floured board and start making *piroshki* as above.

Yields 20 piroshki

BLINY

5 cups milk	¼ pound butter
2 yeast cakes	3 eggs, separated
4 cups white flour	½ teaspoon salt
5½ cups buckwheat flour	½ teaspoon sugar

This recipe should be started the day before you want to serve the *bliny*. Heat the milk until a few drops of it feel warm, but not hot, when tested on your wrist. Dissolve the yeast cakes into it, then stir in the white flour. Mix well and set aside to rise overnight.

In the morning, add the buckwheat flour and beat the mixture with a wooden spoon until it is smooth. Cream the butter with the yolks of the three eggs and add the salt and sugar. Then add the butter mixture to the flour-yeast mixture, blend well and set aside to rise for 3 to 4 hours. Beat the egg whites until stiff, add them to the batter and let rise an additional 10 minutes. Melt some butter in a frying pan and drop a full tablespoon of the batter in to fry, doing 3 or 4 at a time. Do not stir the batter as you use it; take some from the top each time. When the *bliny* are done on the underside (bubbles will form on top), sprinkle them with melted butter and turn them over. Serve with lots of melted butter, add any of a variety of fish, black caviar, red caviar, smoked salmon, pickled herring, etc., depending upon your appetite and taste, and top with sour cream. Sprinkle the top of your final *bliny* with chopped hard boiled eggs, for added taste and decoration. *Serves 6*

BLINCHIKI

1 egg	2 cups flour
2 cups milk	¼ teaspoon salt

Mix the egg with the milk and gradually add the flour and salt. The batter should have the consistency of sour cream. Grease a frying pan or griddle and cook the *blinchiki* as you would pancakes, spreading the batter out so that they are quite thin. Fold in half and serve with butter and jam. These Russian pancakes are good brunch fare and also make a nice teatime snack. *Serves 4*

BLACK BREAD

4 cups rye flour

3 cups white flour

1 teaspoon sugar

2 teaspoons salt

2 cups whole bran cereal

1 tablespoon crushed caraway seed

2 teaspoons instant powdered coffee

2 teaspoons onion powder

½ teaspoon crushed fennel seed

2 packages active dry yeast

2½ cups water

¼ cup vinegar

¼ cup molasses (dark)

1 square dark chocolate (unsweetened)

¼ cup butter

1 teaspoon cornstarch

½ cup cold water

Mix the rye and white flours together. Combine 2⅓ cups of the flour mixture in a large bowl with the sugar, salt, cereal, caraway seed, coffee, onion powder, fennel seed and the active dry yeast, undissolved. Set aside.

In a fairly large saucepan combine the water with the vinegar, molasses, chocolate and butter. Heat until the liquids are warm — the chocolate and butter do not have to melt completely. Gradually add the flour mixture to the liquids, blending thoroughly until smooth. Add enough of the remaining flour mixture to form a soft dough. Turn out on a lightly floured board, cover the dough with a towel and let it "rest" for about 15 minutes. Knead for 10 to 15 minutes, working in more flour if the dough seems sticky, until it is smooth and elastic. Place in a greased bowl, lightly oil the top, cover and let rise in a warm place for about 1 hour, or until doubled in bulk.

Punch the dough down, turn it out on a floured board and divide it in half. Shape each section into a ball about 5 inches in diameter. Place each ball in the center of a well-greased 8-inch round cake pan, cover and let rise in a warm place until doubled again — about 1 hour.

Bake the bread for 45 to 50 minutes, or until done, in 350°F oven. Remove from the pans and brush the tops with a little melted butter, if desired. (This results in a softer crust.) Cool thoroughly on wire racks.

An optional touch is possible which gives the bread that glazed finish you may have seen in bakery Russian bread. A few minutes before the bread is done, combine the cornstarch and cold water and cook, stirring constantly, until the mixture boils and for about a minute thereafter. As soon as you take the bread from the oven, brush the cornstarch mixture over the tops of the loaves and return them to the oven for an additional 2 or 3 minutes. Remove from the pans and cool on wire racks. *Yields 2 loaves*

PERFECT ENDINGS

To me, *plombir* is one of the most festive of all desserts. This is because I remember as a child seeing it served at a Russian restaurant, probably for some very festive occasion. There was a background of *balalaika* music, the waiters wore those high-collared satin blouses that are so colorful and effective, and the *plombir* was carried aloft on a huge silver tray, the frozen mound itself topped with intricate spirals of glistening spun sugar. The spun-sugar topping is not done so often today, but *plombir* is still served both in restaurants and in homes, and it stands very nicely on its own.

Russians are also great fruit eaters, and one of their favorite desserts, *kissel*, is a sort of fruit pudding. It may be made with almost any kind of fruit. Apricot *kissel* is my personal favorite, but it is also excellent with raspberries or cranberries.

Paskha is the epitome of Russian Easter, and probably thousands of pictures have been painted and photographs taken of the pyramid-shaped *paskhas*, always accompanied by tall, dome-shaped *kulichi*. There are many varieties of *paskha* and each family has a favorite. My own favorite is a vanilla *paskha* with a base of hazlenuts: when it is served you get a scoop of both flavors.

It is fun to have a *paskha* mold, and they may be ordered by mail from The Balboa Crystal and Book Store, 443 Balboa Street, San Francisco, California 94118, among other places. Since the cost is minimal, by all means send for one if you want to be authentic. But, on the other hand, don't let the lack of a mold stop you. An excellent *paskha* can be made in a quart-sized plastic ice cream container. Make 3 or 4 holes in the bottom of the container with a hot icepick or fork, so that the liquid will drain off.

A great deal has been written about making *kulichi* and most of it is more than a little intimidating. It *is* difficult to make; that is to say, it is time consuming. But it isn't quite true that the whole thing will collapse right in the oven if anyone so much as walks across the kitchen floor! *Kulichi* can be purchased at Easter in Russian bakeries and food shops in San Francisco, but a large number of Russian-American women still make their own. It is, they admit, a full day's job — which is why they usually make it in quantity and give some of it as gifts. It freezes very well, and keeps for a long time even without freezing.

PLOMBIR

5 egg yolks	**¼ to ½ cup candied fruit, diced**
1 cup sugar	**2 cups heavy cream**
½ cup light cream	

Beat the egg yolks and the sugar together until they are well blended and frothy. Add the light cream and mix well. Cook it over a medium heat, without bringing it to a boil, until it makes a thin custard and coats a spoon. Strain and place in a fairly deep bowl. Let cool, then freeze for about 2 hours until it reaches the consistency of a thick mush. Add diced candied fruit to taste. Use different kinds, cherries, pineapple, etc., to get a variation in colors. Whip the heavy cream and blend it with the original mixture. Pour into a mold, if desired, cover and freeze. At serving time, turn it out on a platter and garnish it with fruit, candied, fresh or canned, and additional whipped cream, if desired. (Maraschino cherries make a pretty decoration.)

Serves 6

APRICOT KISSEL

1 pound dried apricots   1½ teaspoons lemon rind, grated
½ cup sugar   Cornstarch

Cover the apricots with water and let them stand for several hours to soften them, or prepare according to package directions.

Drain, measure the liquid and add enough cold water to make 6 cups of liquid. Cook the apricots in the liquid until the fruit is tender. Put the apricot mixture in the blender and whirl until you have a nice smooth pureé. Return to the saucepan, measuring as you do so. Add the sugar and lemon rind, and let simmer for about 10 minutes. For each 2 cups of the mixture, dissolve 1 tablespoon of cornstarch thoroughly in enough cold water to make a thin paste and gradually stir it into the hot fruit mixture. The consistency should be like that of a cornstarch pudding. Bring to a boil, remove from the heat and let cool. Spoon into individual serving dishes, chill thoroughly and serve topped with whipped cream.

For variations try cranberries, raspberries, peaches, apples, any kind of fruit. Cook until it is tender and then pureé it. Start with ½ cup of sugar and sweeten to taste. Test until you have reached the desired sweetness. Cook the fruit and sugar together as before, then add the cornstarch and water. Finish cooking, chill and serve with whipped cream.   *Serves 4 to 6*

RED WINE SAUCE

2 cups dry red wine	¼ teaspoon cinnamon
4 tablespoons sugar	⅛ teaspoon cloves

Combine these ingredients and let them simmer together over a very low fire for about 10 minutes. This is a good sauce with any kind of bland pudding, like blancmange or tapioca, and is also good on ice cream. Serve it hot over puddings; cool it before serving on ice cream.

RASPBERRY PUDDING

2½ cups canned red raspberries	1 tablespoon sugar
4 teaspoons quick-cooking	1 teaspoon vanilla
tapioca	½ pint sour cream
Red food coloring	1 tablespoon flour
2 eggs	

Drain the raspberries into a saucepan and reserve the fruit. Add the tapioca to the juice and boil slowly for 10 to 15 minutes, or until the tapioca is clear. Add enough food coloring to make the mixture a deep red. Place the drained berries in an 8-inch glass baking dish and pour the tapioca mixture over them. Cool. Beat the eggs with the sugar and vanilla until they are frothy. Beat in the sour cream and gradually add the flour. Pour the egg mixture over the raspberries — do not stir it in — and bake at 325°F for about 1 hour, or until the custard is set. Serve topped with whipped cream. *Serves 4 to 6*

DRACHENA

3 tablespoons butter

2 egg yolks

⅓ cup confectioners' sugar

½ teaspoon salt

2 cups sifted flour

2 cups milk

Fruit preserves for topping

Mix the butter, egg yolks, sugar and salt till well blended, then gradually add the flour. Add the milk and stir into a smooth batter. Pour the mixture in a greased quart baking dish and bake at 350°F for about 30 minutes. Serve warm with fruit preserves.   *Serves 4 to 6*

RUSSIAN CREAM

1 tablespoon gelatin

1 cup heavy cream

1 cup sugar

1 teaspoon vanilla

Soak the gelatin in ¼ cup cold water, then dissolve it with ¼ cup hot water, and stir in a few tablespoons of cream. Beat the rest of the cream until stiff, gradually adding the sugar and vanilla. Pour in the gelatin mixture while still beating the cream. Pour into a mold and chill until set.   *Serves 4*

BLACK BREAD CHARLOTKA

1 loaf pumpernickel or black bread	1 cup sugar
¼ pound butter	1 egg yolk
5 apples	1 cup milk

Cut the crusts off the bread and slice it so that, when placed in a loaf pan, it will completely cover the sides and bottom. You will use about half of the bread for this. Butter the pan and line it with these strips. Cut the remainder of the bread into small pieces, pour a table-spoon of melted butter over them and toast in a 350°F oven for a few minutes.

Core and peel the apples, and cut them into small pieces. Melt 2 tablespoons of butter in a saucepan, add the apples and the sugar, and cook until the fruit is soft. Stir in the toasted bread. Turn into the bread-lined pan. Mix the egg yolk and the milk, pour it over the fruit mixture, cover with foil and bake at 375°F for 30 minutes. Serve with whipped cream. *Serves 6*

ORANGE JELLY

5 large oranges   1 cup sugar
1 lemon   Water
1 tablespoon gelatin

Grate the rind of one of the oranges. Cut the other oranges and the lemon in half and scoop out the pulp. Save the rinds. Boil the grated orange rind with 3 cups of water and the sugar for 10 minutes. Add the gelatin, which has been dissolved in ¼ cup water. Put the orange and lemon pulp into the blender and pureé it. Add to the rind and gelatin mixture. Let cool. When slightly thickened, fill the orange halves with the mixture and chill. Serve with whipped cream.   *Serves 8*

HONEY MOUSSE

4 large eggs, separated
1 cup honey

1 teaspoon orange or lemon
   rind, grated

Beat the egg yolks and the honey together until they are thoroughly blended and frothy. Stir in the rind. Whip the egg whites until very stiff. Gently fold them into the egg-honey mixture. Fill individual dessert glasses and chill. *Serves 4 to 6*

SMETTANIK
(Jam Tart)

2 tablespoons seedless
   raspberry jam
2 tablespoons cherry jam
1½ cups ground hazelnuts or
   almonds
Milk for moisture

2 egg yolks
3 tablespoons sour cream
1 teaspoon cinnamon
1 bottom pie crust and
   lattice strips

Mix the jams. Moisten the nuts with a little milk, then add to the jams with 1 egg yolk, the sour cream and cinnamon. Line a pie dish with pastry. Fill with the jam mixture and cover with lattice strips of pastry. Brush the pastry with egg yolk for a glaze. Bake at 425°F for about 25 minutes, or until nicely browned. *Serves 6 to 8*

SOUR CREAM SOUFFLÉ

Soufflé

2 cups sour cream   ¼ cup sugar

2 tablespoons flour   Rind of 1 orange, grated

4 eggs, separated   Bread crumbs for topping

Sauce

2 cups red wine   ½ teaspoon cinnamon

3 tablespoons sugar   ⅛ teaspoon cloves

Mix the sour cream and flour, and cook until slightly thickened. Separate the egg yolks and beat in, 1 at a time. Add the sugar and orange rind. Beat the egg whites until they are stiff and fold into the batter. Grease a 2-quart baking dish and sprinkle it with bread crumbs. Fill with the batter and bake at 350°F for 25 minutes, or until set. To make the sauce, combine the wine with the sugar and spices and simmer for 5 minutes. Pour over the warm soufflé and serve. *Serves 6*

YABLOCHKO

6 apples	1 cup red wine
½ cup brown sugar	Hazelnuts for topping
½ teaspoon cinnamon	Heavy cream for topping

Peel and core the apples but do not slice them. Fill the center of each with some of the brown sugar mixed with the cinnamon. Place in a glass baking dish, cover the bottom of the dish with boiling water, and bake at 400°F for 15 minutes, basting frequently with the syrup in the dish. Pour the red wine over them and bake for another 15 minutes, or until the apples are soft, continuing to baste them occasionally. Remove from oven, sprinkle sliced toasted hazelnuts over them and serve them with heavy cream.   *Serves 6*

CHESTNUTS WITH WHIPPED CREAM

1 pound chestnuts	1 cup heavy cream
1 cup sugar	Whole chestnuts for garnish

Boil the chestnuts for about 20 minutes. Drain, then shell them and sieve through a meat grinder or ricer. Add the sugar and place in a serving dish. Chill. Whip the cream and pour it over the chestnuts. Garnish with a few whole chestnuts or marrons in syrup, if desired.

Serves 6

WALNUT SOUFFLÉ

½ pound walnuts, shelled   1 cup sugar
5 eggs, separated   ½ cup medium cream

Grind the walnuts. Add the beaten egg yolks, sugar and cream. Cook, stirring constantly, until the mixture is thickened. Do not let it boil. Strain through a sieve and put in a buttered baking dish. Beat the egg whites until stiff and fold them in. Bake at 400°F for 10 minutes and serve immediately. *Serves 4 to 6*

WALNUT CRUMB TORTE

10 eggs, separated   Seedless raspberry jam for
2 cups sugar   filling
1 pound walnut meats, ground   1 cup heavy cream or
1 cup dry white bread crumbs,   ¼ cup confectioners' sugar
    finely ground
2 tablespoons orange rind,
    grated

Beat the egg yolks until thick and frothy. Gradually add the sugar, nutmeats, bread crumbs and orange rind. Beat the egg whites until stiff and fold in. Pour into 3 buttered 9-inch layer pans and bake at 350°F for 30 to 40 minutes, or until set and lightly browned. Cool and put the layers together, alternating with raspberry jam or any flavor of your choice. Cover the top and sides with heavy cream which has been whipped until fairly stiff, or dust the top thickly with confectioners' sugar. *Serves 6 to 8*

VATRUSHKA

Dough

2 yeast cakes	2 eggs
8 tablespoons sugar	5 cups flour
¼ teaspoon salt	6 tablespoons vegetable oil
2 cups warm milk	

Filling

2 pounds baker's or farmer's cottage cheese	12 tablespoons sugar
	1 pint sour cream
½ stick melted butter	4 eggs, separated

Dissolve the yeast in a little warm water, mix it with the sugar, salt, milk and eggs, then mix in the flour until everything is thoroughly blended. Pour the oil into the mixture and turn it out and knead the dough for about 10 minutes. Put in a warm place and let rise for 1 to 2 hours, or until double in bulk. Punch down the dough and roll it out on a floured board until it is slightly larger than a cookie sheet. Reserve some dough for top strips. Butter the cookie sheet, lay the dough over it and trim the excess off the edges. Crimp the edges slightly to make shallow sides.

Mix the cottage cheese, butter, sugar, sour cream and the egg yolks with an electric mixer, or beat thoroughly by hand. Whip the egg whites until stiff and fold them into the cheese mixture. Spread the filling evenly across the dough base. Roll the excess dough into thin ropes and lay them over the filling in a trellis pattern. Brush the strips and dough edges with the egg yolk. Bake at 350°F for about 40 minutes, or until nicely brown.

EUGENIA CAKE

4 eggs
2 egg yolks
1 cup sugar
1½ cups self-rising flour
1 orange rind, grated
¼ pound blanched almonds,
  chopped

¼ pound pistachio nutmeats,
  chopped
¼ pound coconut, grated
1 cup raspberry or
  strawberry jam
Confectioners' sugar for
  topping

Beat the eggs and additional egg yolks with the sugar. Gradually add the flour, the orange rind, almonds, pistachio meats and coconut, all of which should be very finely chopped. Pour batter into 2 greased 8-inch pie pans and bake at 350°F for 25 minutes, or until done. Cool. Cover one of the cakes with jam, top with the other one and sprinkle with confectioners' sugar.   *Serves 8 to 10*

NUT CAKE

Milk
1 loaf rye bread, sliced
1 pound walnuts, shelled
4 eggs, separated

1 cup sugar
Confectioners' sugar for
  topping

Soak the rye bread slices in enough milk to cover until saturated, then put through a meat grinder with the shelled walnuts. Beat the yolks of the eggs with the sugar until creamy. Combine with the bread mixture. Beat the egg whites until stiff and fold them into the batter. Butter and flour a 9-inch square baking pan and pour the mixture into it. Bake at 350°F for 30 minutes or until the cake tests done. To test, put a knife blade into the cake and, if it is dry when you pull it out, the cake is ready. Sprinkle with confectioners' sugar.

Serves 8

POPPY SEED CAKE

1 package white cake mix
4 eggs
⅓ cup vegetable oil
1 cup water

1 package instant lemon
    pudding mix
4 tablespoons whole
    poppy seeds

This is a modern San Francisco adaptation of an old Russian favorite. Put all the ingredients in a large mixing bowl and beat with an electric mixer for about 5 minutes. The longer the better, actually. Grease an angel food cake pan, pour the batter into it evenly, and bake at 350°F degrees for 50 to 60 minutes, or until the cake tests done. Sprinkle with confectioners' sugar, or frost with a white butter icing to which just a little almond flavoring has been added.

Serves 8 to 10

TEA CAKES

1 cup butter
½ cup confectioners' sugar
2 ¼ cups flour
¼ teaspoon salt

¾ cup nuts, finely chopped
1 teaspoon vanilla
¼ teaspoon almond flavoring

Cream the butter and sugar, and gradually add the flour and salt. Blend in the nuts and flavoring. Chill the dough. Break into pieces the size of large unshelled walnuts and roll into balls. Grease and flour a cookie sheet, place balls about ½ inch apart, and bake at 400°F for about 15 minutes, or until slightly brown. Roll in additional confectioners' sugar while still warm. *Yields about 3 dozen*

KHVOROST
(Russian Fritters)

3 cups flour, sifted
3 eggs
½ cup sugar
½ teaspoon salt

½ cup water
1 jigger vodka
Vegetable shortening for frying
Confectioners' sugar for coating

Put the flour into a deep bowl and work the eggs into it, one at a time. Add the sugar, salt, water and vodka. Blend to make a dough. Roll out very thin on a well-floured board and cut into strips about 5 inches long and 1½ inches wide. Make a small slit in the middle of each strip, and pull one end through it. Heat vegetable shortening or cooking oil in a deep saucepan or frying pan and fry the strips, several at a time, until they are slightly brown. Drain on paper towels and sprinkle with confectioners' sugar.

MAZURKI
(Fruit Cookies)

1 cup seedless raisins, chopped

1 cup dried apricots, chopped

1 cup walnuts, chopped

1 cup blanched almonds, chopped

1 cup glazed fruit, chopped

1 cup strawberry or raspberry jam

2 eggs

Rind of 1 lemon, grated

2 cups flour

Combine all the ingredients except the flour, then sprinkle the flour over the fruit and mix thoroughly. Spread the dough out about half an inch deep on a greased cookie sheet or large baking pan and bake at 300°F for about 35 minutes. Cut into diamond shapes while still in the pan. *Yields about 4 dozen*

ALMOND MAZURKI

½ pound butter

2 cups sugar

5 eggs

2⅓ cups flour

1 teaspoon vanilla

1 teaspoon almond extract

½ pound blanched almonds, finely ground

Beat the butter until it is soft and pliable, then add the sugar, little by little. Then beat in the eggs, one at a time. Stir in the flour, add the almonds and flavorings. Keep mixing until very well blended. Pour the mixture onto a buttered cookie sheet and bake at 300°F for about 30 minutes, or until done. (The cookies will be ready if a knife blade, inserted into the middle, comes out clean.) Cut into diamond shapes while still warm in the pan, using a very sharp knife.

Yields about 4 dozen mazurki

MY FAVORITE PASKHA

2 pounds baker's (dry) cottage
    cheese
¾ pound sweet butter
5 egg yolks
2 cups sugar

1 teaspoon vanilla or 1 vanilla
    stick cut very fine
1 cup whipping cream
½ cup hazelnuts, ground
Cheesecloth

Force the cottage cheese through a strainer. Then mix in the butter, egg yolks, sugar and vanilla. Divide into three portions and mix each portion with an electric mixer, then put them all together again. Mix until the consistency is *very* smooth and creamy; you should not be able to readily identify the cheese, as such, when you are finished. Whip the cream until stiff, add it to the cheese mixture and blend thoroughly. Reserve about ½ cup of the cheese mixture and blend the hazelnuts into it. Line the *paskha* mold or ice cream container with cheesecloth. The ends should be a little higher than the container. If you use a plastic container, make sure there are small holes in the bottom for drainage. Fill the container with the *paskha* mixture, ending with a layer of the hazelnut *paskha.* Cover with the ends of the cheesecloth and put a small wooden or plastic disk on top, and then a weight — perhaps a full can of fruit. Set in the refrigerator on a glass, or similar object, which has been put into a larger dish. Quite a bit of liquid forms and it must be allowed to seep out at least overnight, preferably for a couple of days. When you unmold the *paskha,* the fine pattern of the cheesecloth will be visible on the surface, whether you have used the traditional mold or a plastic container, and this is the way it should be. If you have a mold, the letters XB, a cross, Easter eggs in a pattern, and perhaps the dove of peace, will also be impressed into the sides of the *paskha.* This is served cold, always accompanied by a slice of *kulich.*   *Serves 6 to 8*

PINK PASKHA

Follow the basic recipe as above, but add a couple of tablespoons of maraschino cherry juice plus about ½ cup chopped maraschino cherries. Omit the nut layer.   *Serves 6 to 8*

FRUIT PASKHA

1 pound unsalted butter	1 teaspoon almond extract
7 egg yolks	1 teaspoon vanilla extract
2 cups sugar	½ cup mixed candied fruit,
2 pounds baker's (dry) cottage	chopped
cheese	1 cup seedless white raisins
½ pint whipping cream	Cheesecloth

Cream the butter until it is soft. Beat the egg yolks until thick and frothy, then gradually beat in the sugar. Blend the yolks and sugar with the butter. Put the cottage cheese through a strainer, gradually add it to the butter-egg mixture and blend very thoroughly. Whip the cream and add it, with the fruit and flavorings. Line the mold with cheesecloth (if you are using ice cream containers, you may need 2 for this amount of *paskha*). Fill them with the cheese mixture, put a weight on top (a can will do) and let drip in the refrigerator for 2 days. Be sure the molds have holes in the bottom.   *Serves 10 to 12*

CHOCOLATE PASKHA

3 pounds farmer's or baker's	1½ teaspoons vanilla
cottage cheese	1½ cups sugar
¾ pound butter	1½ cups heavy cream
¼ pound dark (unsweetened)	
chocolate, melted	

Force the cottage cheese through a strainer, then add the butter, melted chocolate, vanilla, sugar and whipped cream. Mix thoroughly and mold as in the other paskha recipes.   *Serves 6 to 8*

KULICH

½ cup raisins, seedless
¼ cup rum
3 packages active dry yeast
½ teaspoon granulated sugar
1 cup lukewarm milk
2 cups confectioners' sugar
5 to 6 cups flour
1 teaspoon salt
1½ teaspoons vanilla
10 egg yolks
½ pound sweet butter
4½ tablespoons salted butter
½ cup slivered almonds,
 toasted
½ cup mixed candied
 fruits, diced

Soak the raisins in the rum overnight, then drain them on paper towels and set aside. Reserve the rum. Be sure that all the ingredients are at room temperature, and that the fruits and nuts have already been prepared before the actual process begins. Also beat the egg yolks in advance and have them ready. Sprinkle the yeast and the granulated sugar over the warm milk, let it "sit" for 2 or 3 minutes, and then mix thoroughly, adding a little flour. Put it in a warm, draft-free place for about 10 minutes, or until it nearly doubles in volume.

Mix the confectioners' sugar with the flour and salt in a large mixing bowl. Make a well in the center of the flour mixture and pour in the yeast-milk mixture, the vanilla, the beaten egg yolks and the rum. Stir until everything is well blended and the mixture is smooth. Then gradually beat in the unsalted butter.

Gather up the dough, put it on a lightly floured board and knead it, adding up to 1½ cups more flour, a little at a time, until the dough is no longer sticky. Continue to knead until the dough is smooth and elastic. If the dough "squeaks" as you work it, you will know that you are well on the way to success.

Butter a large bowl with 1 tablespoon of the softened salted butter, put the dough in it, dust the top lightly with flour and cover it with a towel. Put it in a draft-free place until it doubles in volume, about 1 to 2 hours. Combine the almonds, candied fruits and the rum-soaked raisins. Sprinkle them with a tablespoon of flour and stir so that it is mixed evenly. Punch down the dough, add the fruit, and then knead the dough until the fruit is well distributed throughout it.

Use a 3-pound coffee can, greasing it with 2 tablespoons of the butter. Spread a tablespoon or so of oil over a sheet of heavy brown paper about 24 inches long and 10 to 12 inches wide and line the sides of the can with it, the oiled side facing inward. (Do not use butter, as it burns.) Let the paper crown extend up over the edge of the can — it may be folded double for added strength. Cut a circle of the brown paper to fit the bottom of the can, cover it with the remaining ½ tablespoon of butter, and insert it buttered side up.

Place the dough in the can, cover it with a towel and set it aside in a draft-free place for about ½ hour, or until it rises almost to the top. Preheat the oven to 400°F and bake the *kulich* on the lowest shelf for 15 minutes. Then reduce the temperature to 350°F and bake 1 hour longer. The top of the cake should mushroom over the sides of the can, so that it makes a sort of dome, to resemble the domes of the Russian Orthodox Churches. Let the *kulich* cool in the can for about 5 minutes. Then remove it, by first cutting the bottom out of the can with a can opener, and then inserting a long knife between the paper and the metal and gently loosening the cake. Carefully slide out the *kulich*, taking care not to break the mushroom top. Place it upright on a wire cake rack and peel off the paper.

The *kulich* may be decorated with white sugar frosting, sprinkled with colored sugar, or it may be topped with a large candied flower or decorated with a variety of flowers. Traditionally the letters XB are written on the side in white sugar frosting. In serving the *kulich*, the top is sliced off first, straight across, and reserved. You then slice as many circles as you want, cutting each in half. Each person is served a half slice of *kulich* with a helping of *paskha,* and each time the *kulich* is cut, the top is replaced. Thus, the decorated crown is the last to go!   *Yields approximately 24 servings*

NA ZDOROVIE!

Vodka, it goes without saying, is the most famous of all Russian beverages. Although many of the Russians in San Francisco have adopted the custom of mixed drinks, American style, on ordinary working days, vodka is still a must on all special occasions — and the Russians have quite a number of special occasions on their calendar!

Often it is served right from the bottle, well chilled — in fact, it must be icy. But it is also "flavored" in a variety of different ways, which make an interesting change and are very easy to accomplish.

Orange vodka is delicious. It is made simply by peeling an orange — in one long strip, if possible, though it isn't essential! — and putting the peel in the bottle of vodka, tightly closing the bottle, and putting it in the refrigerator for at least 24 hours.

Lemon vodka is made in the same way — use the peel from 1 large lemon or 2 small ones to a bottle of vodka.

Vodka may also be flavored with herbs or hot peppers.

TARRAGON VODKA

1 quart vodka	5 black peppercorns
1 branch fresh tarragon	2 cubes sugar

Mix the vodka with the other ingredients, rebottle, and let stand for at least a week before using it.

RUSSIAN TEA

Real Russian tea should be made from "brisk" tea in a porcelain tea pot. It is allowed to steep until it is a strong infusion. At serving time, some of this infusion is poured into glasses or cups, and then mixed with boiling water to the desired strength. In Russia it was served from a samovar at the table. The small pot of infusion sat on top of the samovar, and the samovar itself was filled with the boiling water. Old samovars had a center core in which hot charcoal was placed to keep the water warm. Today, there are very few families in San Francisco who still have and use a samovar, and if they do it is likely to be an electric one.

Tea is served with either sliced lemon or milk. All sorts of jams are popular with the Russians at tea time, and they have small crystal saucers used especially for them. A dish or jar of jam is placed on the table, and each person puts a little of it in his individual crystal saucer, then eats it with a spoon as he drinks his tea.

So . . . we've gone the gamut of Russian cuisine from *zakuski* to *paskha,* with each step along the way a gastronomic delight. If there is truth to the old cliché about the way to a man's heart being through his stomach, perhaps there is even more validity to the thought that through understanding the customs and cuisine of a people one also comes to understand the people themselves.

Na Zdorovie!

INDEX